TRUMP

How to Get Rich

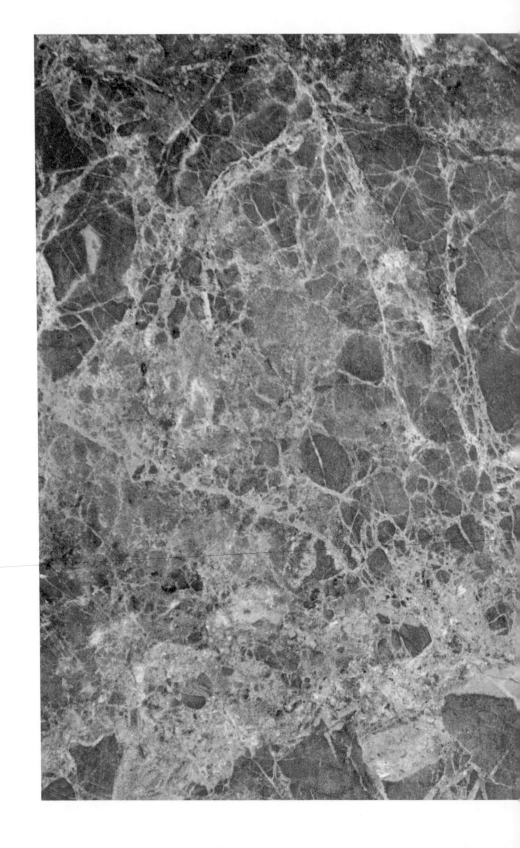

TRUMP

How to Get Rich

Donald J. Trump
with Meredith McIver

RANDOM HOUSE
NEW YORK

All rights reserved under International and Pan-American Copyright
Conventions. Published in the United States by Random House, an imprint
of The Random House Publishing Group, a division of Random House, Inc.,
New York, and simultaneously in Canada by Random House
of Canada Limited, Toronto.

RANDOM HOUSE and colophon are registered trademarks
of Random House, Inc.

Except where noted, all photos courtesy
of Donald J. Trump/The Trump Organization.

ISBN 1-4000-6327-2

Printed in the United States of America on acid-free paper
Random House website address: www.atrandom.com

2 4 6 8 9 7 5 3 1

FIRST EDITION

Book design by Carole Lowenstein

To my parents,
Mary and Fred Trump

The Mother of All Advice

Trust in God and be true to yourself.
—MARY TRUMP, MY MOTHER

*When I look back, that was great advice, concise and wise at
once. I didn't really get it at first, but because it sounded good,
I stuck to it. Later I realized how comprehensive this is—
how to keep your bases covered while thinking about
the big picture. It's good advice no matter
what your business or lifestyle.*

—DJT

Contents

Introduction
Five Billion Reasons Why
You Should Read This Book

A lot has happened to us all since 1987. That's the year *The Art of the Deal* was published and became the bestselling business book of the decade, with over three million copies in print.

(Business Rule #1: If you don't tell people about your success, they probably won't know about it.)

A few months ago, I picked up *The Art of the Deal,* skimmed a bit, and then read the first and last paragraphs. I realized that after seventeen years they still rang true. I could have written these words yesterday:

First paragraph: *I don't do it for the money. I've got enough, much more than I'll ever need. I do it to do it. Deals are my art form. Other people paint beautifully on canvas or write wonderful poetry. I like making deals, preferably big deals. That's how I get my kicks.*

Last paragraph: *Don't get me wrong. I also plan to keep making deals, big deals, and right around the clock.*

It's now 2004, I'm still making deals around the clock, and I still don't do it for the money.

I don't think you should do it for the money, either. Money is not an end in itself, but it's sometimes the most effective way to help us realize our dreams. So if you've got big dreams and you're looking for a way to make them happen, this book is for you.

How to Get Rich. That's what I decided to call it, because whenever I meet people, that's usually what they want to know from me. You ask a baker how he makes bread. You ask a billionaire how he makes money.

Sure, there have been countless how-to-get-rich books written by millionaires. Billionaire authors are harder to find. Billionaire authors with interests in real estate, gaming, sports, and entertainment are rarer still.

And billionaire authors with their own Manhattan skyscrapers and hit prime-time TV series are the rarest of all. I'm pretty sure I'm the only one, though Oprah could give me a run for the money if she ever decides to write another book and get into real estate.

Business Rule #2: Keep it short, fast, and direct. The following pages will be straightforward and succinct, but don't let the brevity of these passages prevent you from savoring the profundity of the advice you are about to receive. These stories and words of wisdom have been distilled from almost thirty years at the top.

So here it comes: The Scoop from The Donald. After you make your first billion, don't forget to send me a thank-you note. You know the address.

Business Rule #3: Begin working at a young age. I did.

PART I

The Donald J. Trump School of Business and Management

In The Art of the Deal, *I mentioned my nemesis and mentor at New York Military Academy, Theodore Dobias, here on my left. Major General John Brugmann is on my right.*

Be a General

I am the chairman and president of The Trump Organization. I like saying that because it means a great deal to me. There are almost twenty thousand members of this organization at this point. I did a print ad once in which I declared, "I only work with the best." That statement still stands.

More and more, I see that running a business is like being a general. Calling the shots carries a great deal of responsibility, not only for yourself, but for your troops. Your employees' lives, to a large extent, are dependent on you and your decisions. Bad strategy can end up affecting a lot of people. This is where being a leader takes on a new dimension. Every decision you make is an important one, whether there are twenty thousand people working for you or just one.

If you are careful when finding employees, management becomes a lot easier. I rely on a few key people to keep me informed. They know I trust them, and they do their best to keep that trust intact.

For example, when I need to know something about my casinos and hotels in Atlantic City, I know I can call up Mark Brown, my CEO, and get a fast and informed answer. If I call Laura Cordovano over at

Trump Park Avenue and ask about sales, she'll give it to me exactly as it is. If I call Allen Weisselberg, my CFO, he'll tell me what I need to know in twenty words or less. My senior counsel and *Apprentice* adviser, George Ross, can do it in ten words or less. Find people who suit your business style and you'll have fewer problems to deal with as time goes on.

Good people equals good management and good management equals good people. They have to work together or they won't work together for very long. I've seen good management get by with mediocre people, and I've also seen excellent people get stuck in the mires of bad management. The good managers will eventually leave, followed by the good workers, and you will be left with a team that gets along because they're all mediocre. Save yourself time by getting the best people you can. Sometimes this can mean choosing attitude over experience and credentials. Use your creativity to come up with a good mix.

Creative people rarely need to be motivated—they have their own inner drive that refuses to be bored. They refuse to be complacent. They live on the edge, which is precisely what is needed to be successful and remain successful.

One of my former employees was in charge of a new project. He had done a thorough and acceptable job, but I felt that something was missing. It wasn't *fantastic,* which, knowing his capabilities, it should have been. I decided to challenge his creative ego by mentioning that it was fine but seemed to lack inspiration. I politely asked him whether he was genuinely interested in the project and suggested that perhaps that might be the problem.

Well, the guy went ballistic on me. He was deeply insulted.

And, as you can probably guess, the revision he turned in was terrific. The difference between the first draft and the final version was incredible. I didn't slam the guy because he was usually demanding of himself and had never let me down. But I had to give him a jolt.

Generals motivate their soldiers; they inspire them when it is necessary. They do the same for their highest-ranking officers. We all need a boost now and then. Learn how to tailor your method to the personalities you are managing.

Keep the big picture in mind while attending to the daily details. This can seem like a balancing act, but it is absolutely necessary for success in running a company.

Stay Focused

In the 1980s, I was riding high. After learning the essentials of real estate development from my father, Fred, a builder in Queens and Brooklyn, I'd become a major player in Manhattan, developing Trump Tower, the Grand Hyatt Hotel, and many other top-tier properties. I had a yacht, a plane, a bestselling book.

One magazine headline said, EVERYTHING HE TOUCHES TURNS TO GOLD, and I believed it. I'd never known adversity. I went straight from Wharton to wealth. Even in down markets, I bought properties inexpensively and made a lot of money. I began to think it was easy.

In the late eighties, I lost focus. I'd fly off to Europe to attend fashion shows, and I wasn't looking at the clothing. My lack of attention was killing my business.

Then, the real estate market crashed. I owed billions upon billions of dollars—$9.2 billion, to be exact. That's nine billion, two hundred million dollars. I've told this story many times before, but it bears repeating: In the midst of the crash, I passed a beggar on the street and realized he was worth $9.2 billion more than I was. I saw a lot of my friends go bankrupt, never to be heard from again.

The media had me for lunch. *Forbes, BusinessWeek, Fortune, The Wall Street Journal, The New York Times*—they all published major stories about my crisis, and a lot of people seemed to be happy about it.

I'll never forget the worst moment. It was 3 A.M. Citibank phoned me at my home in Trump Tower. They wanted me to come over to their office immediately to negotiate new terms with some foreign banks—three of the ninety-nine banks to whom I owed billions.

It's tough when you have to tell a banker that you can't pay interest. They tend not to like those words. An ally at Citibank suggested that the best way for me to handle this difficult situation was to call the banks myself, and that's exactly what they wanted me to do, at three o'clock on a cold January morning, in the freezing rain. There were no cabs, so I walked fifteen blocks to Citibank. By the time I got there, I was drenched.

That was the low point. There were thirty bankers sitting around a big table. I phoned one Japanese banker, then an Austrian banker, and then a third banker from a country I can no longer remember.

In *The Art of the Deal*, I had warned readers never to personally guarantee anything. Well, I hadn't followed my own advice. Of the $9.2 billion I owed, I'd personally guaranteed a billion dollars. I was a schmuck, but I was a lucky schmuck, and I wound up dealing with some understanding bankers who worked out a fair deal. After being the king of the eighties, I survived the early nineties, and by the mid-to-late nineties, I was thriving again.

But I learned my lesson. I work as hard today as I did when I was a young developer in the 1970s.

Don't make the mistake I did. Stay focused.

Maintain Your
Momentum

William Levitt, the master builder of Levittown, taught me the true meaning of "momentum."

In the 1950s, he was the king. No detail was too small for his attention. He would personally collect stray nails and extra chips of wood from building sites to make sure his construction crews used all available materials.

He sold his company in 1956 to ITT for $100 million, which is equivalent to billions today. Then he made some terrible mistakes.

He retired.

He married the wrong woman.

He moved to the south of France and lived on the Riviera with his new boat and his new wife.

One day, ITT called. The executives in charge of the conglomerate had no aptitude for home building. They had bought huge tracts of land but didn't know how to get them zoned. So they sold it back to Levitt, who thought he'd gotten a great deal.

He went back into business. And he proceeded to go bankrupt.

I saw William Levitt at a cocktail party in 1994, two weeks before he died. He was standing by himself in a corner, looking defeated. I didn't know him well, but I approached him, hoping to acquire some wisdom from the master. "Mr. Levitt," I said, "how are you doing?"

"Not good, Donald, not good." Then he said the words I'll never forget. "I lost my momentum. I was out of the world for twenty years, I came back, and I wasn't the same."

No matter how accomplished you are, no matter how well you think you know your business, you have to remain vigilant about the details of your field. You can't get by on experience or smarts. Even the best surgeons need to be retrained regularly, to stay current on the latest research and procedures.

No matter what you're managing, don't assume you can glide by. Momentum is something you have to work at to maintain.

My loyal assistant, Norma Foerderer.

Get a
Great Assistant

Surround yourself with people you can trust. I often say it's good to be paranoid, but not when it comes to your home team.

Ask God for a great assistant. No joke. A great one can make your life a whole lot easier—or, in my case, almost manageable. Norma Foerderer has been with me for twenty-three years. If you want to know what a great guy I am, just ask her. But not on a Friday.

Handling me, the office, and several hundred calls a week isn't easy. She's as tough and smart as she is gracious. She's also indefatigable, which helps a lot if you work for me.

My phones are so busy that I require two executive assistants, and they never stop. They alone handle, on the average, more than 1,250 calls a week. They are not only efficient and fast, but also very pleasant and beautiful young women.

You don't have to be beautiful to work for me—just be good at your job. I've been accused of admiring beautiful women. I plead guilty. But when it comes to the workplace, anyone who is beautiful had better have brains, too. You need competent people with an inherent work ethic. I'm not a complacent person and I can't have a complacent staff. I move forward quickly and so must they.

Once, I wanted to know how fast a new employee could work, so I told him I was leaving in fifteen minutes and needed something done within that time. I wasn't actually going anywhere, but, sure enough, I had what I needed in fifteen minutes. Machiavellian? Maybe, but both of us learned something that day.

One final piece of advice on assistants, which I learned from experience and which, I admit, may not be as relevant to your career as it's been to mine: Find a receptionist who can speak English. We had a breathtaking European beauty out front who could easily rival Ingrid Bergman in her heyday, but I discovered that her ability to recognize well-known people in the United States was limited to myself and maybe President Bush. She wasn't so familiar with the likes of Hugh Grant, Reggie Jackson, George Steinbrenner, Jack Welch, Paul Anka, Mohamed Al Fayed, Regis Philbin, or Tony Bennett. Their calls never got through to me and their names were placed on her "psycho list."

But you should have seen her. What a knockout. She's since moved on to better career opportunities, but we'll never forget her. Neither will anyone who ever called in. Or tried to.

Remember:
The Buck Starts Here

Set the standard. Don't expect your employees to work harder than you do. In my case, I don't have to worry about that, because I work seven days a week and love almost every minute of it. But also realize that your company will sometimes function as an extended and dysfunctional family. It's only natural, considering that people often spend more waking hours with coworkers than they do with their families.

A visitor in my office once mentioned that the goings-on there reminded him of a family fight in progress. I will admit that the volume level gets high now and then, and he wasn't far off in his assessment. But if you want smooth sailing every day, move to the Mediterranean.

Winners see problems as just another way to prove themselves. Problems are never truly hardships to them, and if you haven't got any problems, then you must not have a business to run.

Regard your company as a living, breathing organism, because that's what it is. Those figures you see on your spreadsheets will reflect the health of that organism. Watch out for bad cells while allowing good cells to flourish.

Growth is an indication of life, so keep your organization moving forward at all times. Having a passion for what you do is crucial. If you can't get excited about what you are doing, how can you expect anyone else to? If your employees can see and feel your energy, it is bound to affect them.

Don't intimidate people. If you do, you'll never get a straight answer from anyone, and you'll be defeating your own purpose. I keep my door open, and my people know I'm available as well as approachable. We don't have chat-fests, but whatever needs to be done gets accomplished, and quickly.

Remember that your organization is *your* organization. That sounds simplistic, but, bottom line, it's your ball game. The strategy is up to you, and so are the results. Remember Harry Truman's famous words, which he kept on his desk in the Oval Office? THE BUCK STOPS HERE. I keep a similar quote on my desk. It reads: THE BUCK STARTS HERE.

Don't Equivocate

If you equivocate, it's an indication that you're unsure of yourself and what you're doing. It's also what politicians do all the time, and I find it inappropriate, insulting, and condescending.

I try not to do it. Fortunately, I don't have to try too hard at this one, because I've been known to be on the blunt (and fast) side at times, which is good.

I once asked an executive in my organization to give me a synopsis of a new development we were considering. He'd been to the city in question, had spent some time there, and had done some careful investigating. He went on to describe the merits of the site, the pitfalls, the good things, the bad things, the pros, the cons—on and on in great detail. He must've talked for ten minutes straight. Judging from what he was telling me, there were just as many reasons to drop the project as there were reasons to jump right in and get going. It was like a tied game with no overtime.

I asked him more questions, and we ended up exactly where we were before. He was on both sides of the fence at once and didn't seem to want to take a stand either way. This guy had a lot of experience and a good track record, so finally I asked him what he thought of the project in ten words or less.

"It stinks," he said.

He had eight words left, but he didn't need them.

Ask Yourself Two Questions

1. Is there anyone else who can do this better than I can?
That's just another way of saying: Know yourself, and know your competition. If your competition is better than you are, you need to offer some quality they lack.

2. What am I pretending not to see?
We can all get swept up in the euphoria of a creative moment, or what former president Richard Nixon's speechwriters used to call "the lift of a dream." Before the dream lifts you into the clouds, make sure you've looked hard at the facts on the ground.

Bullshit Will
Only Get You So Far

I think it's funny that the phrase most closely associated with me these days is "You're fired," because, the truth is, although I've had to fire people from time to time, it's not a big part of my job. I much prefer keeping loyal and hardworking people around for as long as they'd like to be here. There's a wonderful lady in her nineties, Amy Luerssen, who worked for my father and still reports to work every day at our Brooklyn office. Here at The Trump Organization, Helen Rakotz has worked for me from the day I moved to Manhattan, and she still puts in long hours every week. She is eighty-two.

Once I delayed firing someone for two years because this guy always had such a great line of bullshit every time I came close to the topic. No matter what was going on, he had some huge deal lined up that was just about to come through.

He managed to string me along for two solid years, and I believed him every time—or wanted to. Finally, I was forced to realize that his claims were bogus, but I gave him every chance before finally axing him.

Unless your boss is a total sadist, he (or she) doesn't want to fire you or cause hardship to your family. If you think you're in danger of being fired, take control of the situation and ask your boss for a meeting.

Make sure you ask for the meeting at the right time. Tell your boss you want to make sure you are communicating and doing your job to everyone's satisfaction.

Of course, if your boss is a sadist, or just a lousy communicator, you've still got a problem. In that case, fire your boss and get a better job. There's no sense in trying to cope with a bad situation that will never improve.

I never try to dissuade people from quitting. If they don't want to be here, I don't want them to be here, either. No one has ever come to me with an ultimatum. People see how it works here, and if it doesn't suit them, they move on. Sometimes it happens quickly. A qualified and experienced receptionist worked here for a grand total of six hours. She realized right away that the pace just wasn't suited to her, and she very politely told us so and left. I appreciated her quick thinking and efficient decision-making skills. She'll have a successful career somewhere else.

Every New Hire Is a Gamble

Some people give such great interviews that you're ready to make them vice presidents on the spot, until you realize that their true talent is simply giving a great interview. That's why, in a sense, every new hire is a gamble.

Impressive credentials don't always add up to a great performance or a good fit. Nonexistent credentials don't necessarily mean a no-talent. Being circumspect helps a lot and keeps you from being surprised. People can offer an interesting mix of pros and cons. Time will do the weeding out for you. All you have to do is pay attention.

What I look for in employees is a sense of responsibility that goes beyond what is merely sufficient. Some people do the bare minimum, and some people will actually be concerned about the organization as a whole. They see themselves as having a direct relationship to the success or failure of the company they work for. They believe they are important, and their work shows it. If you can instill this sense of worth in your employees, you will have a tip-top team working for you. People who take pride in their work are the kind you want to have around—and the kind I like to keep around.

I especially like employees who spend—and, more important, save—the company's money as if it were their own. Companies suffer when employees don't make enough of an effort to control costs. The employees who feel a personal responsibility for their budgets, who view the company's bottom line as an extension of their own personal savings account, are often the ones who get the best results. If you let your boss know that you're watching out for his or her bottom line, you'll always be appreciated.

I respect employees who can think on their feet. So does George Ross, my senior counsel. His assistant, Carole Berkowitz, was helping out at the front desk one day when she received a call from a stranger who said she was about to commit suicide. Carole deemed the call credible and took a few moments to listen to the distressed woman.

Carole asked her where she was from, and the woman replied that she lived in Southern California, not far from the beach. Carole responded, "You live in California? Near the beach? Do you know how cold it is in New York today? It's eight degrees outside! And that's without the windchill. I almost froze just getting to work. If I were you, I'd go out right now, take a long walk on the beach, and sit in the sun for a while. That's what I'd do if I were you." The woman instantly calmed down and thanked Carole for being so nice to her.

That's the kind of person we like to have around.

A certain amount of personal ambition is necessary, but not to the point where it undermines the common goal of the company. If your group can't work together, you won't accomplish much. I don't like backstabbing. It's not necessary, and it's insulting to me. I have eyes and ears and instincts, too. I can assess people and situations for myself. If people have time to be petty, it's an indication they're not busy enough with their work.

You can't expect to be a valuable employee if you don't make yourself valuable. Think about it: What do you contribute to the welfare of the organization? Are you instrumental in keeping it humming and moving forward? Do you work wholeheartedly or halfheartedly? Are you just going through the motions and hoping no one will notice?

The only person you ever fool is yourself. You can't fool others, even though you might *think* you can.

A lot of people say they're going through the motions because their position isn't challenging or rewarding and there's no room to grow. It's a dead-end situation. That might very well be. If so, look elsewhere for a company that could offer you a promotion in your particular area of interest or expertise. There are times when you should move on, and situations in which the only way up is out.

Ideas Are Welcome,
but Make Sure
You Have the Right One

If you run a company, make yourself accessible to your employees. If they feel they can bring ideas to you, they will. If they feel they can't, they won't. You might miss out on a lot of good ideas, and pretty soon you might be missing a lot of employees.

I allow people to run their ideas by me. I don't have a lot of time, so they have to be prepared and succinct. I'm sure that's the protocol of any busy CEO. So if you're going to be bold enough to present your idea, make it as clear as possible, and don't take it casually. Think of it as a presentation that could cost you a lot of money if you were to lose the client. Your boss's time is important, and you won't win any points by wasting it.

Learn to recognize the fine line between being pushy and being intelligently assertive. It can be an issue of timing—pay attention to what's happening around you and pace yourself according to that rhythm. I try to develop a tempo when I'm working. Someone who interrupts it is not going to receive a warm welcome.

Also, remember this: The boss has the big picture; you don't. So if your idea doesn't meet with hurrahs, it could very well be that a similar idea is already in development or that your idea is not in step with plans that have already been made. This shouldn't discourage you, because your initiative will always be noticed. But recognize when *not* to press an issue, and don't expect a lengthy explanation of why.

I like people who don't give up, but merely being a pest is detrimental to everyone. Once again, fine-tune your discernment. Know when to ease up. Keep your antennae up for another idea and a more appropriate opportunity. Sometimes we hesitate with good reason.

There was one former employee who I liked a lot, but he reminded me of a jumping bean. He couldn't keep still for more than three seconds at a time. Even riding in the car with him became an ordeal, because being in an enclosed space seemed to warm him up even more and then he'd really get going. I finally learned to avoid him as much as possible, and that's too bad, because he was a great guy. But enough is enough. Too much will cause people to tune you out—or wish that you would move to another state. Last I heard, the jumping bean was living in Montana. I only hope they have enough space there to contain him, and every time I hear about UFO sightings in Montana, I have to laugh. I know who it is.

One last thing: If your boss says no to an idea, pay attention. Most likely, there's a good reason. No one disregards a terrific idea. It just might not be the *right* terrific idea for the company you're with. Maybe you're meant to go off on your own as an entrepreneur. Let that be an indication to you. It could be the beginning of your career, rather than the end of it.

Focus on the Talent
Instead of the Title

People who work for me know there's a lot more to me than my public persona. I'm not one-dimensional, and if you realize that the people around you aren't either, you'll be utilizing the hidden potential that just about everyone has. Whether they want to use it or not is up to them to a certain extent, but it's also up to a leader to recognize it or at least to give it a chance to unfold. Most people don't like to stagnate, and if you want to keep your company moving forward, look around you now and then for fresh possibilities within your organization. Never let someone's job title be the sole indication of their worth.

People at The Trump Organization have transcended their positions on many occasions. Matthew Calamari, the executive vice president of operations, started as a security guard. After getting to know Matthew, I realized he had a lot more to offer than his job title warranted, and he has proven me right. He's a dedicated and trustworthy worker, and any CEO in his right mind would want to have him around. As an executive VP, he is in charge of building operations and runs my entire security organization. He is in charge of major building projects, with his brother Michael and Andy Weiss. Their most notable

With Matthew Calamari, an executive vice president at The Trump Organization.

recent accomplishment is the new building on the site of the former Delmonico Hotel at Park Avenue and Fifty-ninth Street. I'm calling it Trump Park Avenue. Catchy, right?

Vinnie Stellio, who was hired by Matthew Calamari, started as my bodyguard and is now a vice president. He has just what it takes to be an effective executive, which was clear to me, if not immediately to him. Vinnie would often drive executives, architects, and contractors up to Westchester to look at developments I was building. Now they report to him. I am perhaps the largest owner of land in Westchester County, and now it's Vinnie who keeps his eye on it all.

John Tutolo, president of Trump Model Management, our modeling agency, started as a booker and now has what many guys would consider a dream job.

Meredith McIver, who made the writing of this book a pleasure instead of a headache, started out as a media assistant. I recognized that her talents encompassed much more. Of course, it takes talent to deal with me and everyone else every day (but especially me). I could have hired an outside collaborator to help me with this book, but why spend time looking outside the organization when you have all the people you need right beside you?

Very often, your resources are greater than you might think. I don't like it when people underestimate me, and I try not to underestimate anyone else, either. People are multifaceted, and it's important to let them function in a way that will allow them to shine. Most people would rather succeed than fail, but sometimes the leader has to be the catalyst for putting "success" into their personal vocabulary.

In other words, try to see beyond a person's title. You can find talent in unlikely places.

Meredith McIver, Rhona Graff, and Norma Foerderer of The Trump Organization.

Manage the Person, Not the Job

I once heard a story about a guy who owned an advertising agency. There was one writer who drove the other writers crazy because he would appear to be doing nothing in his office. He made no attempt to look busy.

Finally, his colleagues complained to his boss about his laziness. The boss suddenly perked up and asked, "How long has he been this way?"

One of the other writers answered, "For weeks and weeks! He sits there and does zip. It's like he's in a coma."

The boss said, "I want all of you to be quiet and not to disturb him, and every now and then ask if you can get him some coffee or some lunch or run some errands for him."

Needless to say, the employees were deflated and started grumbling. Then the boss explained his rationale: "Listen, the last time he was acting this way, and the time before that, he came up with ideas worth many millions of dollars. So when I tell you not to disturb him, I have a reason for it."

People have different ways of achieving results. I enjoy figuring out how each of my key employees excels. If people are your resource, you'd better try to learn something useful about them. Being able to do so is what makes a good manager a great one.

Some people respond well to the fear factor. Ever hear this exchange?

Question: "How long have you been working here?"
Answer: "Ever since they threatened to fire me."

Well, it applies to some employees. Fortunately, I seem to attract people who enjoy working, but now and then a few slugs will show up, and the loss of face (or job) can be a good motivator for many.

That said, it will always work against you to demoralize your employees in any way. I can be tough, but most people will admit I'm fair. You can crush people if you don't weigh your words carefully. Your power as a leader should be used in the most positive way, which sometimes calls for a great deal of restraint as well as patience. I have to laugh when I hear people say, "I can't wait until I'm the big shot so I can order everyone around." It doesn't quite work that way.

Abraham Lincoln made an appropriate remark that is pertinent to management: "Nearly all men can stand adversity, but if you want to test a man's character, give him power."

Keep Your Door Open

I'm always taken aback when people say, "Oh, he's got it made," as if that's the end of the conversation about a person. They seem to be saying that the person can just check out and coast because he's already arrived.

To me, arriving means something is about to begin. Graduation from college is a beginning, not an ending. Each success is the beginning of the next one.

Learning is a new beginning we can give ourselves every day.

A know-it-all is like a closed door. Everyone who knows me knows I keep the door to my office open. It's symbolic of the way I choose to think, and it's the way I operate. My father was much the same. He once said to me, "You know, the more I learn, the more I realize I don't know. I think that has kept me young at heart more than anything else." It was an offhand comment, a quiet realization he mentioned to me one day while he was reading, but it has stuck with me for decades.

Every day is a reminder to me of how much I don't know. Everything I learn leads me to something else I didn't know. Fortunately, I don't pride myself on being a know-it-all, so every day becomes a new

Looking for a raise? Come on in.

challenge. People ask me what keeps me going, and this is probably the closest answer to the truth. If I end the day without knowing more than I did when I woke up, it makes me wonder: What did I miss out on today? Am I getting lazy? I am a disciplined person, and this thought alone can get me going.

We've all heard the phrase *creature of habit*. That can be good or bad, depending on your habits. I've cultivated the learning habit over the years, and it's one of the most pleasurable aspects of my life. Everyone in my family knows I'm big on education—not just Ivy League education, but all education, and for people of all ages. That also applies to me, and while I got very good grades at school, I do not have time to be a scholar. Still, it's something I aspire to in my quiet time. Possibilities unfold. The world opens up.

My sister Maryanne introduced me to the writings of Aldous Huxley. He was such a learner that when he was faced with near-total blindness as a young man, he learned braille and continued his studies anyway. His description of this predicament had not a trace of self-pity. In fact, he mentioned that it had offered some benefits: He could now read in bed at night and his hands would never get cold because he could read with his hands under the covers.

Learning begets learning. I'd rather be stimulated than passive.

You can't wear a blindfold in business. A regular part of your day should be devoted to expanding your horizons.

We live in a big world, and it is important for us to be aware of cultures other than our own. I have always lived in the United States, but I make an effort to be informed about other cultures. That's easy to do in New York City, the most diverse and exciting place on earth.

Someone who had been living abroad for a few years told me, upon returning home, that a frequent comment about Americans is that you always know exactly where we're coming from. The flip side of this is that we rarely know where *anyone else* is coming from. We're very much up to snuff about our own national events, but we are less aware of what's happening in other countries. All of us need to pay more attention to events outside our own realm. We are connected to each other in so many ways—politically, commercially, socially. Perhaps one of the reasons I've been able to sell and rent apartments to people of so many foreign nationalities is that I've made an effort to understand where they're coming from.

Learn something new, whether you think you're interested in it or not. That's the opposite of having a closed mind—or a closed door. I can thank my father for the example he set. It was the key to his remaining young and dynamic into his nineties. It can do the same for you, if you make the effort.

Think Big and
Live Large

This is the final rule of the Donald J. Trump School of Business and Management. Once you have mastered it, you are ready to graduate.

It's a big world. There's a lot we don't know, which means there's still a lot to be discovered and a lot to be accomplished.

The possibilities are always there. If you're thinking too small, you might miss them.

In some ways, it's easier to buy a skyscraper than a small house in a bad section of Brooklyn. Either way, you'll probably need financing, and most people would rather invest in a great building than a dilapidated duplex on a dangerous street. With the skyscraper, if you hit, at least you hit big. And if you don't hit, what's the difference between losing $100,000 or hundreds of millions of dollars? Either way, you've lost, so you might as well have really gone for it.

I've read stories in which I'm described as a cartoon, a comic book version of the big-city business mogul with the gorgeous girlfriend and the private plane and the personal golf course and the penthouse apartment with marble floors and gold bathroom fixtures. But my cartoon is real. I am the creator of my own comic book, and I love living in it. If you're going to think, think big. If you're going to live, live large.

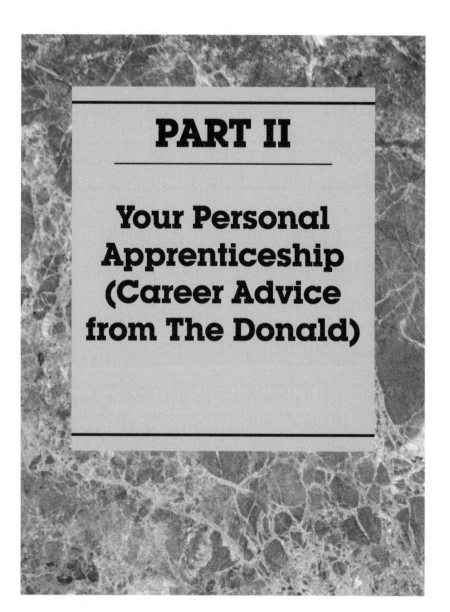

PART II

Your Personal Apprenticeship (Career Advice from The Donald)

Take Control of the Job Interview

I've had some interesting experiences with job interviews over the years. Norma Foerderer is a good example. I wasn't too sure about her after her first interview. It had nothing to do with her skills. But she seemed a little too prim, like she belonged on some family sitcom as the ever-so-proper type. I didn't think she could handle it here, or that she would fit with my style.

Norma persisted, seeming to recognize a good match better than I did. Little did I know how deceptive first impressions could be. Norma was actually as far from fluff as you could get. So, I thought, *Okay, maybe.* Her abilities were superior to those of anyone else I had seen. As it turned out, I called her back on the same day her mother died, but Norma gave me an offer I couldn't refuse: She'd work for me for one month at a low salary just to see whether we clicked. No strings attached.

I thought, *Aha!* She'll never last anyway, and I can decide on someone else in the meantime. After one month with me, she'd be outta here for sure. The hoity-toity type just won't fly, except out the front door.

Needless to say, I underestimated Norma completely. I was duly humbled and, I must add, grateful for being so. She was persistent and committed to getting the job, and she did it with elegance.

Ask for Your Raise at the Right Time

When it comes to your career, certain moves should not be made without careful consideration of the old and very apt saying "Timing is everything."

For example, if you've decided to ask for a raise, look around first. So many times, employees who I like very much do the dumbest things when it comes to conversations about their salaries.

Jason Greenblatt, a young and brilliant lawyer who works for me, is terrific at everything he does, but one day, I swear, he must have been wearing blindfolds—and earplugs.

I was having an especially tough, vicious, terrible, miserable day that seemed never-ending to me and to everyone else. It was a grand-slam rotten day. No one could possibly have mistaken it for anything else.

Late in the afternoon, by which time I had had enough, I heard a polite knock on my door. I yelled out "WHAT?" in my most exasperated tone. Jason nonchalantly entered my office, completely ignoring my angry welcome, and proceeded to ask me for a raise.

I could not believe a lawyer as smart as Jason could make such a dumb move. I use his real name only because Jason knows how much

I like and respect him, despite his incredible faux pas. But I have to tell you that I was ready to kill him. Was he *joking*? It's amazing, but he wasn't. He was dead serious. I couldn't believe it.

Did he get a raise? Not that day. He almost got fired for stupidity, except that I told him to get out before I really lost my temper. I also told him that although he might be brilliant, his timing for certain things needed work—and that maybe he ought to start paying attention to what was going on around him. I remember thinking to myself, *Did I really hire such a person?* But as I said, it had been a rough day.

Jason is still with me, and he gets lots of raises because he's great at what he does. But now he always waits for sunny days, blue skies, and puffy white clouds on the horizon before approaching me. I told you he was smart.

The best way to ask for a raise is to wait for the right time. It also indicates to your boss that you have a certain amount of discernment and appreciation for what he might be going through himself. I need my people to be plugged in to what's going on with me.

What impresses me most about people is their work ethic. A certain amount of swagger is okay—it's just another form of enthusiasm—but, bottom line, I look for results. When I mentioned to a salesperson that I had to cut her salary because she'd made no sales in nine months, she just about went nuts. But some things are common sense. What would she do if she had a nonproductive salesperson on her own roster?

If you knew your company was scheduled to give a major client presentation at 3 P.M., would you approach your boss at 2:45 to ask for a raise?

Money, like comedy, is all about timing.

Be Tenacious

The Art of the Deal contained a chapter called "West Side Story," about my acquisition of the West Side yards, a hundred-acre property fronting the Hudson River from Fifty-ninth Street to Seventy-second Street. The chapter title was a deliberate double entrendre, as I knew that the popular musical *West Side Story* had taken ten years to put together. Its creative team had included no less than Leonard Bernstein, Jerome Robbins, Stephen Sondheim, and Arthur Laurents, so whenever I experienced setbacks or delays on my West Side project, I would remind myself that I had some very illustrious company.

It's now seventeen years later and it's still a work in progress, but the example set by the architects of *West Side Story* has served me well. You don't create a classic overnight.

I'm calling it Trump Place. It's a $5-billion project, the biggest development ever approved by the New York City Planning Commission. When it's done, Trump Place will have 5,700 residential units and more than five million square feet of commercial space. So far, four towers have been completed and are occupied, and two additional buildings are under construction. When we're done, there will be a total of sixteen buildings on the site.

Trump Place is a good example of why tenacity is crucial in business. I bought the property in 1974. We've hit snags along the way and made many changes over time, but for more than thirty years, we've persisted. At times, just about every executive will appear impatient, but to build something that endures, you have to take the long view.

Recently, an employee told me that the pastor of her church had used Trump Place as an example of what a firm foundation should be, whether it be in faith, family, or, as in my case, buildings. The pastor, whose church was near the construction site, would watch each building go up and marvel at the immensity of the work. Each building could be a hundred stories high, he said, considering the meticulous foundation work.

My publisher sent me an inspiring book by Bill Shore called *The Cathedral Within*, which celebrates the commitment and hope necessary to build something that endures. It might be a cathedral like the one in Milan, which took five hundred years to build, or it might be a community organization or a business.

Paul Davis, the man developing Trump Place for me and my partners, is a true cathedral builder. I have rarely seen anyone work so hard or so diligently—Saturdays, Sundays—he's there at all hours, paying close attention to every impeccable detail of the layouts, room sizes, and the quality of the fixtures. He's one of the big reasons for our success.

Some things are worth waiting for. For me, Trump Place is one of those things: Sixteen beautifully designed buildings on the Hudson River. A twenty-five-acre park. The Upper West Side as a backyard. This could prove to be my finest contribution to the city of New York. Time will tell, but I'm in no rush, and I won't stop until I'm done.

Golf is a brain game, and practice makes perfect.

Play Golf

I made a lot of money on the golf course before I ever went into golf as a business. I found solutions to problems, new ideas for ventures, and even a new career. Golf has a way of giving you an equilibrium that you can't always find in the office.

Doing what you love will always make you a winner, and after spending many happy hours on golf courses, I decided to build some of my own. I am now one of the busiest golf course developers in the United States, with two award-winning, internationally acclaimed courses fully operational and two more in the works.

My first course, the Trump International Golf Club in Palm Beach, Florida, has been home to the ADP LPGA championships for three years. When I first decided to develop the most beautiful golf courses possible, I did some research and got in touch with the most respected designers in the business—the Fazio family. Just as Michelangelo had an affinity for sculpting marble, some people have an affinity for sculpting land. In this case, Jim and Tommy Fazio designed a dream come true for any golfer, not only visually, but in terms of playability.

The course opened in 1999. With its waterfalls and landscapes unique to Florida, Trump International Golf Club is already a landmark course in the state—and the best course in Florida.

My second course was Trump National at Briarcliff Manor in New York. We moved three million yards of earth, the largest land excavation ever in Westchester County, and it was worth it. We were also dealing with stone, which was used for walls and a spectacular waterfall on the thirteenth hole—a 101-foot cliff of black granite quarried from the property—which pumps five thousand gallons a minute. The walls were built by my very talented stone mason, Frank Sanzo. Membership costs $300,000. I think it's a bargain.

My third golf course is Trump National Golf Club, in a sumptuous area of New Jersey known as Bedminster. It is being designed by the master golf course architect himself, Tom Fazio. Three times, *Golf Digest* has named Fazio the Best Modern Day Golf Course Architect, and when you see this course, you'll know why. It will be long, big, and beautiful, and I am involved daily in the design and construction. Additional plans for this property, formerly owned by automaker John DeLorean and located in the heart of New Jersey's horse country, will include a second course and a world-class clubhouse designed in the colonial mansion style.

I don't want to limit my golfing to the East Coast, so in 2002 I bought a course along two miles of the Pacific Ocean. What was formerly known as Ocean Trails in Palos Verdes will now be known as Trump National Golf Club, Los Angeles. The course had fallen into disrepair under its previous owners—the eighteenth hole fell into the ocean—so I'm rebuilding it with legendary golf course architect Pete Dye. We're also planning to build luxury estate homes on the property. When completed, this course will be the best in California.

When we announced the deal, the *Los Angeles Times* reported, "As he has so many times before, Trump has spotted a trend to tap." True, but mostly I was following my instincts and my interests.

Building golf courses is not a big business for me and it's unlikely that I will ever do another one. I want only the best.

Sometimes I will sell memberships while I am hitting balls on the

Dave Anderson, Joe Kernen, me, and Ron Howard at the opening of Trump National Golf Club in Briarcliff Manor, New York.

practice range. People approach me and hand me checks. One recent day at my Florida course, a group of four wealthy friends came to me with checks of $300,000 each. I said to myself: *Not bad; I'm playing a game I love and going home with $1,200,000 in my pocket.*

I realize that some of you don't care much about golf. Golf is one of those things that has aficionados, just as opera has diehard fans who will fly around the world to catch a certain performance. To people who don't know or like opera, that seems absurd.

I can't make you love golf, but, believe me, once you've had the opportunity to play on a beautiful course, it could turn you into an enormous fan, or even a passionate player, no matter how poorly you hit the ball.

If anyone had told me twenty years ago that I'd become a dedicated golf course developer, I would have sent them out of the room for being ridiculous. But golf has a transforming power. It's a brain game. Yes, there is skill and technique involved, but, just as important, it requires concentration and assessment.

It's a great way to improve your business skills, to learn how to maneuver. It can even be equated with learning how to negotiate, which is an art in itself.

Golf is also, in essence, a solitary game. Being an entrepreneur, even within a large company, is a solitary game.

Ultimately, the rule here is not just to visit one of my golf courses (though you would be wise to do so) but to turn your passion into profit. The results of that passion will reward you in more ways than you ever could have expected.

Passion is enthusiasm on a big scale. It is all-encompassing and consuming. People with passion never give up because they'll never have a reason to give up, no matter what their circumstances may be. It's an intangible momentum that can make you indomitable.

Take out the passion and you will have a fizzle or, perhaps, an okay product at best. Add the passion and you will be in a rarefied realm that every other "passionista" will recognize—and one that every person would like to enter.

A friend of mine is a member of what I call "the lucky sperm club"—born into a wealthy family. He followed his father to Wall Street, but he was a total failure. He didn't like it, and he couldn't do it. Meanwhile, he became increasingly involved in his Connecticut country club. He was named the head of the greens committee and took on the lead role in rebuilding the golf course. He loved it and was great at it. The club held a dinner for him out of gratitude for his volunteer work. I asked him, "Why don't you do this for a living? You're not for Wall Street. You're getting eaten alive there." He told me his family wouldn't understand if he quit a serious job to work on golf courses.

Well, two years later he took my advice, quit the Wall Street job, and is now working full-time at renovating golf courses. He says he loves getting up in the morning, and he is doing better than ever.

Of course, you don't have to learn how to play golf to have a satisfying career. But no matter what you do, you must be passionate about it.

There's no place like home.

Brand Yourself and
Toot Your Horn

I was originally going to call Trump Tower by another name—Tiffany Tower, for the famous jewelry store next door. I asked a friend, "Do you think it should be Trump Tower or Tiffany Tower?" He said, "When you change your name to Tiffany, call it Tiffany Tower."

We've all seen the power of a brand name, especially quality brand names. Coco Chanel became world-famous eighty years ago by naming her first perfume Chanel No. 5, and it's still going strong in a fiercely competitive market. Her fragrance, as well as her name, has become timeless. She proved that the right ingredients can create a legend.

Trump has become a great brand name, due to my rigorous standards of design and quality. We all admire Rolls-Royce cars, and I see every one of my ventures as being just that elite. Being a stickler has paid off, because my buildings are considered to be the finest in the world. That may sound like bragging, but it's also a fact. I've never been one to confuse facts with fiction. In 2003, *Chicago Tribune* real estate columnist Mary Umberger attributed the sales for Trump International Hotel and Tower in Chicago to "The Trump Factor." Umberger reported: "The sales velocity surprises even experienced real-estate players, who told me at the sales inaugural that they doubted Trump would gain enough momentum because Chicago's luxury market was—and is—in a lull."

Some people have written that I'm boastful, but they're missing the point. I believe in what I say, and I deliver the goods. If you're devoting your life to creating a body of work, and you believe in what you do, and what you do is excellent, you'd better damn well tell people you think so. Subtlety and modesty are appropriate for nuns and therapists, but if you're in business, you'd better learn to speak up and announce your significant accomplishments to the world—nobody else will.

When I'm setting the price for a luxury apartment, I consider a lot of factors—the market, the location, and the competition. Then I set my own standards. Once, when some top-of-the-line apartments weren't selling, I upped the prices, way over the competition. They started selling immediately.

I view my work as an art form and approach it with the same intensity and ego as any ambitious artist would. I never planned on becoming a brand name, but the fit of my aesthetic nature with each product I became involved with has resulted in an expanding network of interests. The success of the Trump name worldwide has been a surprise.

It's been a good surprise. For example, using my name on a building carries with it a promise of the highest quality available and at least a $5-million price tag. That's just for the name, because it will be worth it to the developers, and they know it. That building will be up to my standards. When I remember the line from Shakespeare's *Romeo and Juliet*—"What's in a name?"—I have to laugh. What's in a name can be far more than either the Bard or I ever could have imagined.

We've all noticed the ascendancy of brand names and the power they have, from Levi's to Louis Vuitton. Some people are against this widespread branding, seeing it as another form of labeling. I see it as a viable outlet for creativity.

If you're on the brink of success in your career, some snob might ask you dismissively, "You don't want to become a brand name, do you?" Anyone who asks you that does not have the big picture in focus—and they are usually just envious.

I can get a project off the ground in no time now, whereas an unknown developer would require many months, if not years, to get something going. The number of people I employ to get a project finished reaches into the thousands, and those people would not have a building to work on without a developer to give them a job. Commerce and art cannot function independently—they must work together. That is the beauty of a successful brand name.

If there is a downside to being a well-known name, it is that you become an easy target. The media needs to tear down what it builds up; that's just part of journalism—stories are about heroes and villains, or success and failure. If you're a brand name, they're going to take a shot at you. It comes with the territory, and I've learned to live with it. As we say on *The Apprentice:* It's not personal. It's business.

Fortunately, if you have the critics who matter on your side, reading the newspaper can be a lot of fun. Herbert Muschamp, the architecture critic for *The New York Times,* is a scholar and an authority when it comes to buildings. To receive a compliment from him has an intrinsic value that will never diminish. When he wrote an article on Trump World Tower and described it as "a handsome hunk of a glass tower," I was very honored. Here's more of what he wrote:

> Although Donald Trump prefers to publicize the aggressive side of his nature—it's the manly thing to do—he is also the only beauty freak at large in New York City real estate development. . . . It's not surprising that unofficial approval of Trump's building should come by way of the Museum of Modern Art. The tower embodies the Miesian aesthetic through which the Modern's design department's taste was initially formulated—I

hope Trump sticks with this material. Trump does better when he ignores his critics than when he pays attention to them.

So don't be afraid to toot your own horn when you've done something worth tooting about.

And don't believe the critics unless they love your work.

Go with Your Gut

Being an entrepreneur is not a group effort. You have to trust yourself. You may have superb academic credentials, but without instincts you'll have a hard time getting to—and staying at—the top.

This is one of those gray areas that remain an enigma even to those who have finely honed business instincts. There are inexplicable signs that can guide you to or away from certain deals and certain people.

For example, within a few seconds of meeting Mark Burnett, the creator of *The Apprentice,* I knew he was one hundred percent solid, both as a person and as a professional, which is a remarkable accomplishment in the entertainment industry.

On the other hand, I've met people that I have an aversion to for no particular reason, and while I try not to be judgmental, I have reason by now to trust my gut. Carl Jung said our conscious minds use only five percent of our brain power for daily functioning. If we can learn to tap into that unconscious, subconscious, and dormant ninety-five percent, the results can be amazing.

Be Optimistic, but Always Be Prepared for the Worst

There are a lot of ups and downs, but you can ride them out if you're prepared for them.

Learning to expect problems saved me from a lot of wasted energy, and it will save you from unexpected surprises. It's like Wall Street; it's like life. The ups and downs are inevitable, so simply try to be prepared for them.

Sometimes I'll ask myself why I want to take on some new, big challenge. A substantial loss is always a possibility. Can I handle it if it doesn't go well? Will I be asking myself later, *Why did I ever do that? What was I thinking?* I'm actually a very cautious person, which is different from being a pessimistic person. Call it positive thinking with a lot of reality checks.

Look Closely
Before Changing Careers

In 2000, I thought about running for president of the United States as a third-party candidate. I proposed some sensible ideas: tax cuts for the middle class, tougher trade deals, a ban on unregulated soft money in campaigns, comprehensive health care reform. I formed an exploratory committee and met with Reform Party leaders, but in the end I realized I was enjoying my business too much to run for office.

Remember the rule I mentioned earlier about how you shouldn't equivocate? That may work for business, but in politics, you usually have to watch your words. I'm too blunt to be a politician. Then, there's my long-held aversion to shaking hands. (More on this in a moment.) Had I entered the race, I wouldn't have been very popular. Even during the few months I was considering candidacy, I noticed that people began to treat me differently—in a more reserved, less friendly way. Before, I had been The Donald, someone they would wave and smile at. Suddenly, it was a different ball game, and it didn't seem like much fun to me. One guy I had been friendly with for years saw me at Le Cirque and for the first time in my life called me "Mr. Trump." He had always called me "Donald." That was a real heads-up.

A lot of successful businesspeople think they can apply their management skills to politics, but I've noticed that only a select few, like Michael Bloomberg and Jon Corzine, succeed. Most others lack the temperament for it.

There's a larger point here, beyond the obvious ones about not confusing your talent for office politics with a gift for electoral politics. Anyone with more than a little curiosity and ambition will at some point be tempted to try a different challenge on new terrain. Take the risk, but before you do, do everything you can to learn what you're getting yourself into, and be as sure as you can that you've got the right mind-set for the job.

Avoid the Handshake
Whenever Possible

Some business executives believe in a firm handshake. I believe in *no* handshake. It is a terrible practice. So often, I see someone who is obviously sick, with a bad cold or the flu, who approaches me and says, "Mr. Trump, I would like to shake your hand." It's a medical fact that this is how germs are spread. I wish we could follow the Japanese custom of bowing instead.

The worst is having to shake hands during a meal. On one occasion, a man walked out of the restaurant's bathroom, jiggling his hands as though they were still wet and he hadn't used a towel. He spotted me, walked over to my table, and said, "Mr. Trump, you're the greatest. Would you please shake my hand?"

I knew that if I didn't shake his hand, he'd be saying terrible things about me for thirty years. I also knew that if I agreed, my own hands would be loaded with germs or whatever the hell he'd carried out of the bathroom. I had a choice.

In this case, I decided to shake hands, because I was a little overweight at the time and knew that if I shook his hand I wouldn't eat my meal—and that would be a good thing.

Pay Attention
to the Details

If you don't know every aspect of what you're doing, down to the paper clips, you're setting yourself up for some unwelcome surprises.

I once read about an esteemed brain surgeon in San Francisco who was known for being fanatical about detail and organization. He would go over the components of an upcoming surgery in his head as he jogged every morning. He'd visualize every detail, as if to remind himself of everything he'd learned, every difficulty and complication he might encounter.

He wasn't known for his bedside manner, but he was the best. If I had to have brain surgery, he's the kind of surgeon I'd choose. But you don't have to be a brain surgeon to pay attention to the details.

Connect with Your Audience (The Art of Public Speaking, Part I)

One of the problems with my schedule lately is that I am unable to accommodate most of the requests I receive for public speaking. I happen to enjoy giving speeches. I know some people dread the thought of having to give a presentation in a boardroom, let alone appearing before thousands of people. Not me. I get so much energy from my audiences that it is always fun.

I'll bet a lot of you are wondering whether I'm making that up to sound like I'm not afraid of anything. It's possible I'm forgetting a few stressful moments. Years ago I was probably nervous about facing an audience, but I got over it. Being afraid of speaking in public is something you can conquer. The following pointers can be applied by people who find presentations, whatever the size of the audience, to be a roadblock on their highway to success.

It helps if you are a naturally gregarious person. My driver, Tony, recalls a time when I was going to deliver a speech. When we were about five minutes away, I asked Tony what I was supposed to be talking about that night. Tony couldn't hide his shock. He said, "Boss, don't you *know?* There are twenty thousand people waiting for you."

Telling it like it is.

I said, "Yeah, but I've been busy. I'm sure it will be okay." I was trying to reassure him.

No go. He said, "Where are your notes? Didn't you make any notes?"

I said, "I'm making some now."

Tony was looking at me through the rearview mirror with an expression of astonishment. I think he was checking to see whether I was kidding. I wasn't.

I'd been asked to give the speech by Anthony Robbins, the best-selling author and self-help guru. I had been paid a great deal of money for the speech, but I'd never asked how many people I would be speaking in front of. As I was leaving the office to go to Philadelphia, my secretary told me I would be speaking at a basketball arena, the Wachovia Center, and that there would be approximately twenty thousand people there. I said, "You've got to be kidding. I've never spoken before twenty thousand people before!"

That situation could cause panic in some people. Instead, I thought about my audience not as a massive group of people just waiting to judge me, but as individuals who might be there because they're interested in something. Then I started thinking about what people are interested in and the kinds of questions people like to ask me.

I was ready. I suddenly had a gut feeling that we were all in for a great time.

Leaving an ashen-faced Tony in the car, I hopped out, ready to embrace the experience. Somehow the audience picked up on my energy and got much more than a speech. They got give-and-take that no one who was there will soon forget. We had a hilarious time, and we walked away having learned a few things as well.

Tony Robbins turned out to be a terrific guy. Until I met him, I didn't believe in him or trust him, but that was only because I was getting my information secondhand. Having gotten to know him and his wife, I now wholeheartedly endorse him—he is out to do good and help people. His seminars are absolutely a happening, and after our successful experience in Philadelphia, I agreed to make ten more appearances.

All in all, it was a valuable lesson in public speaking: Think about your audience first. The rest will fall into place.

Granted, having useful information to convey will help, too. But tuning in to *people* is the first step. I'm good at that, and I don't have to try too hard. Even in my office, with a few people around, the conversation will never be one-sided. I like to involve everyone and hear what they have to say.

So: Involve your audience. They will appreciate being included.

Cover These Eleven Bases
(The Art of
Public Speaking, Part II)

When you're speaking, it helps to be prepared. That may sound funny after what I've just told you, but if you read every day, you will already be prepared—maybe not for the fine points you are specifically speaking about, but usually we are asked to speak about something we are experts at or at least familiar with. Cover your bases mentally. Imagine yourself being in the audience. What are you looking for? Being able to trade places with the audience can open you up to a lot of ideas. Have examples and references in mind to back up your statements, and make them as vivid as possible for your listeners.

Notes can sometimes function as a useful reference point, especially if you're speaking to a large audience. If you're prepared, no one can tell that you're using them. Ideally, you don't want to read a speech. For some reason, no matter how good your delivery is when you read a speech, it's usually boring. Everyone sees that you're reading it and it's never quite the same as delivering it off the cuff. Notes offer the best of both worlds: They keep you focused and moving in the right direction without turning you into a stiff.

Be a good storyteller. People like stories, and they'll remember them. A speech shouldn't become a lecture. Humor goes a long way, and it will remind you and everyone else that we've all got a lot of things in common. Storytelling is a skill, so work on it. It's helpful to listen to comedians. The good ones can teach you the art of great timing.

Think about the common denominator. How can all of us relate to one another? How can you enable your audience to relate to you and to what you're saying? People see me as a rich and powerful person, but like most people, I also have a daily routine and a family. I get stuck in traffic jams, too. I've known some real gems and some real wackos. I have cranky moments and bad days like everyone else. A lot of your experiences can be understood and appreciated by your audience because they've had them, too. Look for what you have in common and lead with it. You will create an immediate bond, because they will realize they can relate to you.

When you are on the podium, you are the entertainer. People are there to learn something, but also to be entertained. One reason Elvis Presley was such a great entertainer is that he made every effort to tune in to his audience—it was give-and-take all the way. Wayne Newton does that, too. Even people who thought they wouldn't like Liberace became big fans after experiencing his live shows. And nobody did it better than Sinatra.

Some people call it charisma. I call it tuning in and delivering.

Study Regis Philbin. He is relaxed and funny, and he always relates to his audiences. They love him. He's a perfect example of the give-and-take that's necessary for successful public speaking. Regis doesn't just speak—he shares. He's as magnanimous a performer as he is a person. Watch him, pay attention, and you'll learn a lot.

Be able to poke fun at yourself. This will make you accessible to people even if you are up on the stage and in the spotlight. We've all had disasters in our lives, major and minor. To be able to laugh at them in retrospect is healthy and helpful. Use the blips that we all encounter in our lives to your advantage. I remember a particular question-and-answer period that followed one of my speeches, during the time when Ivana and I were going through our divorce and the tabloids were having a field day. The first question was from a guy who asked, "You don't mind if I call you *The Donald,* do you?"

So I responded, "Not if you don't mind if I call you Ivana."

We all had a good laugh and then proceeded to his real question.

Learn to think on your feet. Memorable public speaking involves a good deal of spontaneity. It's a lot like negotiating—you have to focus on your goals but remain flexible. A lot of people are terrific writers but not so great at getting their ideas across orally. Writing is a form of thinking, and so is speaking. The difference is that you don't have time to go back and correct yourself when you're on stage. It's not a first draft and it's not a rehearsal. Be prepared for the performance, because that's what's expected of you.

Listen in your daily life. Every day can be a preparation for a speech or a presentation. Have you ever said to yourself, "I'll have to remember that one" after hearing someone say something particularly clever or unusual? Even offhand comments that you overhear can be useful. Remember them. Make notes if you must. Everything and everyone can become material. I was in the back of an elevator once, behind a group of guys. Their conversation was so vivid, so real, that I tuned in and tried to figure out why they'd captured my attention. Aside from the fact that they had a captive audience for a short amount of time, I realized that their speaking rhythm was syncopated, quick, and to the point. What they were saying wasn't all that fascinating, but their delivery was. They made a normally mundane subject—what they were getting for lunch and how they were getting it—seem interesting.

Have a good time.   It's contagious. If your audience believes you are enjoying what you are doing, they'll enjoy being in your company. If it's an obvious chore to you, forget it and find someone else to speak for you. If you're a busy executive, there's probably someone within your organization who can speak effectively in your place. Sometimes when I'm asked to speak and my schedule won't allow it, I will ask someone who works for me if they'd be interested in filling in. Charlie Reiss, executive VP of development in my organization, was a professor at Columbia University before he came to work for me. He's a dynamic speaker, but I wouldn't have known this if I hadn't asked him to help out when I was in a bind. He has a gift for public speaking because he enjoys teaching and is enthusiastic about what he does. At first I worried he might turn out to be a bit pedantic, considering his background, but he wasn't. Everyone had a good time.

Another important aspect of having a good time: Before you speak, remind yourself that it doesn't matter all that much. Don't feel that the weight of the world is on you. Most of the people in the room don't care how well or poorly you do. It's just not that important. It's merely a speech—not an earthquake or a war. You'll have a better time and be a better speaker if you keep it all in perspective.

That said, public speaking and presentations may be a necessary step on your ladder to success. For quick reference, here's my procedure for discovering a talent you thought you didn't have:

1. Think about your audience first.
2. Get your audience involved.
3. Be prepared.
4. Be a good storyteller.
5. Be aware of the common denominator.
6. Be an entertainer.
7. Be able to laugh at yourself.

8. Think on your feet.

9. Listen.

10. Have a good time.

And, of course . . .

11. Study Regis Philbin.

Change Your Altitude

When I say *altitude,* I'm not referring to my jet. It's my own interpretation of the word *attitude.* I like flying because it gets me where I'm going, fast. Likewise, if you have the right attitude, you can get where you're going, fast.

What's the altitude of your attitude? Is it high frequency or low frequency? Having a high frequency will attune you to a wavelength that exudes confidence and clear-sighted enthusiasm. I'm a firm believer that this is half the battle of any enterprise.

I'm a tough-minded optimist. I learned a long time ago that my productivity was increased by a large percentage simply by learning to let go of negativity in all forms as quickly as I could. My commitment to excellence is thorough—so thorough that it negates the wavelength of negativity immediately. I used to have to zap negativity mentally. By now, it just bounces off me within a moment of getting near me. As you may have heard, I don't like germs. I'm still waging a personal crusade to replace the mandatory and unsanitary handshake with the Japanese custom of bowing. To me, germs are just another kind of negativity.

Negativity is also a form of fear, and fear can be paralyzing. On the golf course, I've heard great athletes tell me that they can't putt. They can hit a ball three hundred yards right down the middle of the fairway, but they can't finish the hole by putting the ball three feet into the cup.

Recently, I played with a man who is terrified of putting. He hit a magnificent 235-yard shot and was seven feet from the cup. Then he looked over at me and said, "Now the hard part begins."

Another friend, also a great golfer, is paralyzed by his fear of losing his ball. Each time we played a hole near a lake, he would look down and say to his ball, "I have a feeling I'll never see you again."

I have told these two guys that they must start thinking positively or they will sabotage themselves.

Very often, negative thinking stems from low self-esteem. You have to work on this yourself. Maybe you've received a lot of hard knocks. I've learned to deal with them because I get knocked a lot. Quickly see them for what they are—knocks. But you don't have to open the door unless you choose to. I've gotten to the point where I see knocks as opportunities and as an insight into whoever is doing the knocking.

One way to chase low altitude away is to think about how fortunate you already are and how much you still have to look forward to. You can better your best day at any time. Very surprising things can happen, but you must—and I repeat *must*—be open to them. How can you fly if you've already clipped your own wings?

I don't have time to encourage as many people as I would like to, but whenever it seems appropriate, I recommend *The Power of Positive Thinking* by Norman Vincent Peale, one of my father's favorite books, and mine, too. Some people may think it's old-fashioned, but what Peale has written will always be true. He advocates faith over fear. Faith can overcome the paralysis that fear brings with it.

I can remember a time when I had a choice to make, when I was billions of dollars in debt. I had to take one of two courses of action: a fearful, defensive one or a faithful, riskier one. I carefully analyzed the situation, realized what was causing the uneasy feeling of fear, and immediately replaced it with blind faith, simply because I had nothing else to go on at the time. Then I resolved that as long as I remained positive and disciplined, things would work out.

There was not much more I could do. I didn't know how it was going to go, but I was determined to move forward, even though it wasn't easy. Within a relatively short amount of time, the situation was settled positively. I learned a lot from that and have since had a better understanding of what courage really is. Without facing my own fear, I would not have known.

When I think of someone who is tough, I also think of someone who has courage. People who persist have courage, because often it's a lot easier to give up. Some of the bravest people I've met are children with handicaps. I'm active with United Cerebral Palsy. What those kids deal with is humbling, but they are enthusiastic and thrilled with every day they've been given.

You've been given a day, too. When you're down, look at it that way. Another day can equal another chance. Sometimes, as obvious as it sounds, we really do have to take things one day at a time. Immediately after the events of September 11, we didn't know what was going to happen, but we all kept going, one day at a time, and we're still moving forward.

Maybe you've gotten to the point where you think you can't get through another day. That's shortsighted of you. You're missing the big picture. You're on the runway, but your fuel supply is the problem. You won't get off the ground without it. Feed yourself some positive thoughts and you can take off at any time.

Ever wonder what makes certain people keep going? I do. Abraham Lincoln encountered a steady procession of setbacks, but he just kept at it. Nothing deterred him. He must have had a lot of faith, because he didn't receive much encouragement along the way. He's an excellent example of someone who never gave up.

The other extreme is the person who seems to run into obstacles with the unerring aim of a marksman. I knew a guy who was remarkably accident-prone. If there was something to run into, he'd find it. If there was a hole in the ground, he'd break his foot by stumbling into it.

Once, he was in such a slam-bang accident that he was hospitalized for six months before being completely patched up. Finally, the day of his release from the hospital arrived and it was decided that he should get an ambulance ride home, just to be on the safe side. As the ambulance was taking him home, it crashed into a car—another spectacular slam-bang accident. My friend was immediately brought back to the hospital, in a new ambulance dispatched to the scene of the disaster. What can I say? Maybe he's just a really unlucky guy. Or maybe he's a loser. I know that sounds harsh, but let's face it—some people *are* losers.

The altitude level of losers is so low that they should walk around in scuba gear all day. They are below sea level on the altitude map. We all know people like that, and they might make great comedians because they have so much material—but first they'd have to learn to be funny. Honestly, I've known people who are such accomplished losers that I think that's what they devote their time to:

How can I be the biggest screwup possible?
How can I prove the born loser *theory to be correct?*
How can I defy the law of probability to make it an absolute *disaster every time?*
How can I achieve a perfect record of total wipeouts?
How far can I get at zero miles per hour?
How can I reach the lowest frequency possible?

How can I operate so that radar could never possibly find me even if I get lost, which I probably will?

These people need a new speedometer.

Get going. Move forward. Aim high. Plan for a takeoff. Don't just sit on the runway and hope someone will come along and push the airplane. It simply won't happen.

Change your attitude and gain some altitude. Believe me, you'll love it up here.

Start Visualizing Positively

Positive thoughts will create positive visuals. Have you ever heard someone say "I can just *see* it!" when they are enthusiastic about something? I know from experience that if I can see something as a possibility, it has a much better chance of happening than if I can't see it happening.

Give your higher self a chance once in a while by giving your possibility quota a boost.

Keep a book of inspiring quotes nearby, so you can change a negative wavelength the moment it descends on you. Here are some of my personal favorites:

> Know everything you can about what you're doing.
> —MY FATHER, FRED TRUMP

> I know the price of success: dedication, hard work, and an
> unremitting devotion to the things you want to see happen.
> —FRANK LLOYD WRIGHT

> A leader has the right to be beaten, but never the right to be surprised.
> —NAPOLEON

"I remember when _I_ was the Donald!"

Cartoon in The New Yorker
(© The New Yorker Collection 1993, Lee Lorenz from
cartoonbank.com. All Rights Reserved.)

Let's avoid subtlety on this one.
—CHARLIE REISS, *Executive Vice President of Development,*
The Trump Organization

He who looks outside his own heart dreams, he who looks inside his
own heart awakens.
—CARL JUNG

Exciting is a dull word for the business we're in.
—FRED TRUMP

You're the only guy who can wear a cashmere overcoat to a baseball
game and get away with it.
—REGIS PHILBIN

Imagination is more important than knowledge.
—ALBERT EINSTEIN

Continuous effort—not strength or intelligence—is the key to
unlocking our potential.
—WINSTON CHURCHILL

I remember when *I* was the Donald.
—DONALD DUCK

Read Carl Jung

I find reading psychology and self-help books useful. Carl Jung's theories fascinate me and keep my mind open to my own—and the collective—unconscious.

Reading his books can also be a good form of self-defense.

There's a lot we don't know about ourselves. Likewise, there's a lot we may not know about everyone else. Jung used the word *psyche* to refer to both the conscious and the unconscious processes. (That's where the word *psycho* comes from, by the way.) I first became aware of Jung through an acquaintance who had endured some extreme ordeals, yet he remained calm. I couldn't fathom where he got this sort of "grace under fire" demeanor, so I asked him, and he told me that Jung's ideas kept him centered.

My friend put it like this: "Donald, I've learned from my experiences. As a safety factor, I very often see other people as a revolver that could be pointed at me. They are the gun. I, however, am the trigger. So I speak and tread carefully. It's an effective visual aid to avoid conflicts, as I was unwittingly among people who were actually psychos underneath their dignified personas. We never know what will trigger another person's killer instinct. It can be something that happened when they were five years old. So avoid being the trigger, and the revolver will not be a threat."

This synopsis of his philosophy made such an impact on me that I immediately started reading about Carl Jung. I'm glad I did, because it helped me in my business as well as in my personal life. We are all evolving human beings, and being aware of this gave me a big boost toward maturity. It also made me less inclined to be surprised by so-called aberrant behavior. I have to stress that I am not cynical, but I am aware. I hate being in situations where I'm asking myself, *How could this have happened?* This reminds me of my favorite quote from Napoleon about being surprised: A good leader shouldn't be.

You have to know yourself as well as know other people to be an effective leader. For me, reading the work of Carl Jung was a step in the right direction. If someone had told me in business school that studying psychology would be important for financial success, I would not have believed it. My friend's story changed that, and I am grateful to him for such cogent advice. The relatively small number of hours I've spent reading Jung have been more than worth it. Start with his autobiography, *Memories, Dreams, Reflections,* and you will be in for a fascinating time while simultaneously fine-tuning your intuition and instincts. You will also gain a technique for seeing into—versus reading into—the people around you. Believe me, this will serve you well on many levels.

The word *persona* has an interesting root. It comes from the Latin word meaning "mask." This, however, is not derogatory. It's necessary. Each of us has a persona. We need it for survival. It's the face we put on for public use, and it can be intentional or unconscious. For example, a salesman who has lost his entire family in an accident is, naturally, dev-astated. But to work effectively with his customers, he must appear cheerful and confident. That's part of his persona. It's a survival device.

The only danger is when people become their personae. That means something has been shut off somewhere along the line, and these people will end up hiding behind the false personality that works professionally. As I am very much in the public eye, this hit home and I gave it considerable thought. Fortunately, I am aware of my public side as well as my private side, and, while I'm not one for hiding much, I know there are several dimensions in which I operate. That's one reason I feel at home at The Trump Organization. The people I work with day in and day out know I'm not entirely a glam guy. They see how hard I work. One person said I am very much like a Mormon, which I took as high praise.

Anyway, reading Jung will give you insights into yourself and the ways in which you and other people operate.

Have an Ego

As you know, this rule has been easy for me to follow. But hear me out—I've got a good reason for it.

Having a well-developed ego, contrary to popular opinion, is a positive attribute. It is the center of our consciousness and serves to give us a sense of purpose. I remember saying to someone, "Show me someone with no ego and I'll show you a big loser." I was trying to stir things up and provoke a reaction, but I later realized the basic idea is on target.

The ego works to keep our conscious and unconscious aspects in balance. Too much either way can be detrimental. No ego means very little life force, and too much means a dictatorial personality. Keep your ego in a healthy balance, for your own well-being as well as for those around you. Strive for wholeness. It's an intelligent approach to life and business.

Understanding how egos work can be a great tool. Did you ever notice how you can deflate an opponent by simply saying, "Yeah, whatever you say . . ."? By doing this, you are gently assuming a no-ego position, which disarms the other person while at the same time taking the wind out of their sails. It gives you the peace of mind necessary to allow you to concentrate on something more important than dealing with someone who is playing God.

Sometimes, rather than confronting a tyrant or a psycho directly, it's more effective to keep the knowledge to yourself and proceed accordingly, behind the scenes.

We've all heard the saying that knowledge is power. The intelligent use of that power is crucial in the business world, and it's just as important in your personal life. Your mind can build castles—just make sure the foundations are in place first. You, and the people around you, will be grateful for that.

Keep Critics in Perspective

In any job, you will be criticized at some point. Let's face it: Nobody but a total masochist wants to be criticized.

There is constructive criticism, and then there is destructive criticism. Here's how to assess both types:

1. First of all, consider the source. Should this person's opinion even matter to you?
2. If it does matter to you, take a few minutes to consider whether anything helpful can result from the criticism. Others can often see things that we have overlooked. Use their keen eyes to your advantage.
3. Critics serve their purpose. Sometimes they serve a larger purpose, and sometimes they serve their own purpose. *American Idol* judge Simon Cowell can be critical of the performers on the program, but he's fair and he's honest, and I don't think *American Idol* would work without him. Simon was nice enough to compliment *The Apprentice* in an interview. "I think it's absolutely fantastic," he told the *Daily News*. "I think [Trump] is superb on the show. He's not hamming it up. He's just playing himself and that's very hard to do on television." As I said, Simon is a fair and honest critic, and I am a fan of his.

4. Everyone has an opinion. In most cases, it's not worth the paper it's written on.

5. If the opinion is worth the paper it's written on, and it's written in a paper people are buying and reading, then realize that if people didn't find you interesting enough for public consumption, they wouldn't be taking the time to criticize you. Think of their criticism as a compliment, proof of your significance.

Homework Is Required
and There <u>Will</u> Be a Test

People who think achieving success is a linear A-to-Z process, a straight shot to the top, simply aren't in touch with reality. There are very few bona fide overnight success stories. It just doesn't work that way.

Success appears to happen overnight because we all see stories in newspapers and on TV about previously unknown people who suddenly become famous. But consider a sequoia tree that has been growing for several hundred years. Just because a television crew one day decides to do a story about that tree doesn't mean it didn't exist before.

In 1955, Glenn Gould, the classical pianist from Toronto, rocketed to international fame by recording Bach's Goldberg Variations. He was young and unusual, but he had already been practicing the piano for close to twenty years. He may have seemed like an overnight sensation to the general public, but anyone who's been working at something for twenty years isn't likely to agree with that assessment.

I have to admit that my knowledge of classical music is limited, but from what little I've read on the subject, I know that the process of becoming a classical musician is a long and demanding one. The amount of practice hours required to master an instrument is astounding, and also never ending. How do they do it? I'm not sure, but I would guess that passion plays a large part.

Every industry and profession has its bottom line for what is required to succeed. If you can't stand to practice every day, being a musician is out of the question. If you hate to exercise, being an athlete is not for you.

In business—every business—the bottom line is understanding the process. If you don't understand the process, you'll never reap the rewards of the process. You'll never last long enough to achieve your "overnight" success.

Part of the process is doing your homework. You have to know what you're getting into first. That was one of my father's strongest beliefs. We've all heard the phrase "You're barking up the wrong tree." It brings to mind a funny image, but in reality it can be embarrassing. Not doing your homework can result in something analogous, so do a few things first to avoid this.

We can learn from our mistakes, but it's better to learn from our successes. When I hear people say, "Well, it was an *interesting* experience," I can usually safely assume they are referring to something that didn't work out the way they'd planned. I don't find my goof-ups to be amusing or interesting.

Can you imagine hearing a surgeon say, "Well, it didn't go quite right, but I sure learned a lot"? I wouldn't want that guy operating on me. The same applies to anyone in business, because if you're in business, it's not just *your* money involved, but very often the money and well-being of others as well. In my business, I can't take chances. If something is not quite right with the design or construction of a superstructure, a lot of people could be injured or killed. I've *got* to know what's going on. Bottom line, it will be my responsibility.

People see the finished product. Wow, a skyscraper! What goes into it is another story. Construction isn't glamorous. It's a serious and often dangerous endeavor. Fortunately, I understood this from my earliest days in the business, so there's a certain gravity in my approach to the construction of any building.

That's where having learned to do my homework comes in handy. It's a necessary requirement, not an extracurricular course to enhance my productivity. Not only do I have to know exactly what I'm doing, but I've also got to make sure I find contractors who know exactly what they're doing as well. That's why I'm tough on them, and that's why I'm equally tough on myself. A lot of lives are at stake in our work. We don't want any "interesting" experiences!

We all know what it's like to pretend to study. There are some courses in school that just don't hold your attention. If you are choosing a career, keep that in mind. What most holds your attention?

Consider a pyramid. Did you ever notice how large and solid the foundation is? Did you notice the carefully graduated levels that eventually lead to the pinnacle? Now turn the pyramid upside down. That's a representation of topsy-turvy thinking. You don't start at the top. You start with the foundation—the stronger, the better.

The world moves along at such a fast clip that we have little patience when things are slow, whether it's the line at a supermarket or Internet access. We've become intolerant of those things that cannot be accelerated or skipped entirely. I can't speed up the foundation work for a building, nor can I expect to play piano like Glenn Gould just because I want to.

Know the limitations as well as the possibilities of everything you do. Find out as much as you can *yourself* about what you plan to do, and don't expect anyone to act as your favorite grandmother in wanting what's best for you. Most people want what's best for *themselves*, not for you. If those people have already spent a great deal of effort on their homework, why should they share it with you?

Listen to a Ping-Pong Game

I learned a long time ago to listen, but to listen judiciously. You can learn a lot from the people around you—you just have to be discerning about the information that comes your way. A lot of the so-called information I receive turns out to be someone's personal opinion. We're all entitled to our two cents' worth, but sometimes that's all it amounts to.

Be aware of the marketplace. Know what's going on now. That's one reason I devote several hours a day to reading. That's how long it takes to both keep up with current events and learn from the greats in history. How can you expect to be successful if your idea of what's happening in the world is vague or nonexistent? That's like saying, "I know that September 11 happened, but I choose not to acknowledge it. It gets in the way of my positive outlook on things." That approach is fine if you're a professional fairy-tale writer.

There's another side to everything, so develop your ability to see it—or even hear it. I once met a young woman from Hong Kong who worked on Wall Street in emerging markets. She had an uncanny ability to predict certain events in the marketplace—it seemed almost like a psychic gift to me.

One day, I asked her how she could be so on target in her work and she likened knowing and predicting the global markets to *listening* to a Ping-Pong game.

At first, I thought she was joking, or perhaps just being evasive, but she went on to explain her theory.

"I'm not kidding you, Donald. When I was growing up, we had a Ping-Pong table in the den, and I could hear the games my brothers would play, sometimes for hours, when I was studying in my room. I discovered that I could discern the tilt of the paddle, and the outcome of the volley, just by the sound of the Ping-Pong ball being hit, and the sound of it landing on the other side of the net. I knew the results, the repercussions, and the recovery that would be required to successfully handle what had been dealt.

"Later, I applied this to my work in emerging markets and found I could often predict what would be happening just by concentrating on world events and thinking of the sound of Ping-Pong balls being hit around the globe. Ping-Pong is really the reason behind my success."

I was astounded. *That's* my idea of tuning in.

I must add that this young woman had all the education in finance that her position required. She was a bright student. What set her apart from everyone else was the way she applied her knowledge and her keen analysis of the game of Ping-Pong to her work. She may even have done this on an unconscious level initially, but tapping into this resource gave her an uncanny edge. The lesson I learned from her story is never to underestimate the power of awareness.

Find out what other people have done to succeed, and then be prepared to do ten times more. There are no guarantees.

Comparing ourselves to others is a waste of time. I've heard people say, "Well, Mr. Lucky had a million dollars before he was thirty and I've worked just as hard as he has." Well, Mr. Lucky has nothing to do with you, your possibilities, your success, or your failure. Don't let anyone else be your yardstick. That's taking power away from yourself in a big way.

You've got your own personal blueprint to attend to. We can't all be Tiger Woods, J. Lo, Bill Gates, or whoever it is you would like to be, and sometimes that's a hard fact to face. You may have already experienced defeat. That happens. It happens a lot! But the fact that you have aspirations to begin with is putting you on the road to success right now. No matter how defeated you may feel, you've still got a chance. But it won't happen by itself. Get to work!

I'll sum up with two of my favorite quotes:

> There are no short cuts to anywhere worth going.
> —BEVERLY SILLS

> The harder I work, the luckier I get.
> —GARY PLAYER

Reflect for
Three Hours a Day

I read an article recently in which European exchange students living in the United States all agreed on one aspect of American life: The noise level here is very high. We seem to avoid quiet moments. Even lapses in conversation are quickly filled with banter or some kind of interference.

It made me realize how much I need a certain amount of quiet time—usually about three hours a day—in order to stay balanced. It's time I use to read and reflect, and I always feel renewed and refreshed by this. It also gives me material to feed my extroverted nature.

For me, the early morning hours are best for this kind of reflection. I'm an early riser, usually up by 5 A.M., which gives me a few hours to read newspapers and magazines of all sorts—local, national, and international.

In the evening, after a black-tie dinner, I'll unwind by stopping at my local Korean grocery for snacks—potato chips and pretzels. That will be my dinner. I rarely get to eat at those black-tie events, and I'd rather have the junk food, anyway.

Once I'm home, I read books—usually biographies. Now and then I like to read about philosophers—particularly Socrates, who emphasizes that you should follow the convictions of your conscience, which basically means thinking for yourself, a philosophy I tend to agree with. It may not make you too popular, but it's essential for lucid thought, and it's a good way to avoid being part of a herd mentality of any sort.

I read as much as I can, but not as much as I'd like, because there are so many constraints on my time. I am grateful for the contribution Oprah Winfrey has made to our country in regard to reading. In my book *The America We Deserve,* I wrote about the deplorable state of reading in this country. Since Oprah decided to do something about it, there has been a noticeable upswing in book sales, and writers are once again considered to be cool people rather than dinosaurs. I cannot thank Oprah enough for what she has done, and I hope every person in this country realizes the positive influence she has had. We all owe Oprah a big thank-you, and I'd like to lead the crowd in saying so.

I like movies and television as much as anyone else, but reading is a form of replenishment for me. The potato chips and pretzels help, too.

Dress for Your Culture

I used to pride myself on buying very inexpensive suits and other clothing. It just didn't make sense to pay thousands of dollars for great clothes when you could buy something for a hundred dollars. Who would know the difference?

Over the years, I've learned that this is wrongheaded. I now buy very high-quality shoes, and they seem to last forever, whereas the cheapos used to wear out quickly and always looked as cheap as the price I'd paid for them. The same is true for suits. These days, I go for Brioni, whose service and attention to detail is second to none. They supplied most of the clothing for *The Apprentice*, so I have tremendous loyalty to them (and I got a good deal). They also make great overcoats.

The way we dress says a lot about us before we ever say a word. To me, dressing successfully means understanding your environment: knowing the culture and making an effort to reflect—and respect—it.

The "look" in Beverly Hills may be attractive, but that same look may be met with scorn on Wall Street. Success is hard enough to achieve without showing up on casual Friday in a three-piece suit. Don't put up unnecessary hurdles for yourself.

Make it easy for people to take you seriously. I would wonder about someone who arrived for a meeting or an interview and was dressed inappropriately for the culture of that particular workplace—for example, a guy showing up at Trump Tower in a cowboy hat, boots, and a fringed cowhide jacket. It's more about culture than style. Be aware of your surroundings and dress accordingly.

Some people can get away with anything. Most people can't. Micha Koeppel, who works at The Trump Organization, usually looks like a Canadian Mountie in full regalia. To look at him, you'd think he was about to lead an expedition through the Rockies. Then again, my buildings are tall, and he scouts the right locations for them, so maybe there's a reason for his getups. It works for him, and he does a good job, so I don't mind.

It's certainly not groundbreaking news that the early victories by the women on *The Apprentice* were, to a very large extent, dependent on their sex appeal. The fact that sex sells is nothing new. However, women are judged harshly when they go too far, so be careful in how you present yourself. If you want to be acknowledged for your intelligence as well as your beauty, don't stand in your own way. Not everyone can tune out a knock-em-dead appearance. Think of how you would like to be perceived, and proceed from there.

I tend to notice what people are wearing only if they look exceptionally well put together—or exceptionally badly put together. It has more to do with style than which designer they may or may not be wearing. As I said, expensive clothing usually looks like it was worth the price.

Have you ever noticed how we tend to pigeonhole people in certain professions by their appearance? It's a form of shorthand to just be able to say "your basic accountant type" or "a typical advertising type" when describing someone. Every profession has a certain look or standard. Just say "banker" and you've saved yourself a hundred words. It's not always fair, but that's how it works.

However, you don't have to be a typical anything.

For example, Frank McKinney looks like a cross between a rock star and a surfer dude. You would never guess by looking at him that he's a real estate entrepreneur who sells ultra-high-end residential real estate in Florida. When he speeds by you on his motorcycle in his Versace vest with his two feet of blond hair blowing in the wind, you can bet he's on his way to a business meeting. But that's Frank's style, and he's very successful.

I'm a conservative dresser due to business considerations and to save time. I enjoy flamboyance in other people—I'm more interested in what a beautiful woman might wear than in anything I might ever put on.

Be aware that your attire can literally become a costume. I've known a lot of terrific-looking scoundrels and a lot of well-dressed bums.

Being tasteful is being tasteful, no matter what line of work you're in. Sure, it helps to have the money to buy great clothes, but a little style can go a long way.

PART III

Money, Money, Money, Money

Here I am on top of Trump World Tower at the United Nations Plaza. I like to check up on things, even without my helicopter.

Be Your Own
Best Financial Adviser

Many people go out and hire financial advisers, but I have also seen a lot of those advisers destroy people.

Athletes, in particular, make a great deal of money at a very young age. Too often, some manager squanders the athlete's fortune and they wind up in their thirties with nothing left but their past glory—and are forced to get jobs just to survive.

A good friend of mine and truly one of the greatest basketball players who has ever lived, Kareem Abdul-Jabbar, was in the NBA for over twenty years, only to find that some bad advice had destroyed much of his wealth. I don't know whether it was theft or stupidity, but it was a shame.

Herschel Walker is an athlete who signed big contracts, with both the USFL and NFL. One day, he came to me and told me he was going to invest in a fast-food franchise. I told him, "Herschel, you are a friend of mine, but if you do that, I will not speak to you again." Because of the relationship we had (and continue to have), he decided not to make the investment. The company went bankrupt two years later. Herschel is now a wealthy man, and he thanks me every time I see him.

When it comes to picking a financial adviser, rely on your own judgment based on what you read in reliable publications like *The Wall Street Journal, Forbes, BusinessWeek,* and *Fortune.* They are usually terrific, even though, on occasion, they say some negative things about me. I'm angry at *Fortune* at the moment—and for good reason—but even *Fortune* sometimes manages to awake from its stupor to report something worthwhile. I'm particularly impressed with an editor there named Geoffrey Colvin, who is also the host of *Wall Street Week* on PBS and has written perceptively about corporate restructuring.

The *New York Post* has developed a truly great business section—and one that is fun to read. Lately, *The New York Times's* coverage of business has gone right to the top!

If you read these financial publications for a while, you will start to pick up on the cadence and get a feel for what's happening in the market, which funds are the best, and who the best advisers are.

Stay with the winners. Often, you will read about somebody who has made money quickly and then relies on one of his friends to invest his fortune. That friend has no track record, and if it weren't for his connection to a rich investor, he wouldn't have any money. Beware of instant stars in the world of finance. Trust the people who do it again and again, and who are consistently ranked high by the four best institutional business media outlets. But trust your own common sense first.

Invest Simply

There are numerous firms that provide comprehensive charts and other information on the best returns from certain financial advisers and funds. Study those charts, not over the short term (maybe they just got lucky) but over a fifteen- or twenty-year period.

Invest with the help of a major firm like Goldman Sachs, Morgan Stanley, Bear Stearns, or Merrill Lynch. These are your hard-earned savings at stake. Don't take unnecessary risks.

Generally there is a reason for success. When you look at legends like Alan "Ace" Greenberg and Warren Buffett and marvel at how good they are, you will likely see that what makes them so successful is the same quality you should apply to every one of your own investments—common sense.

I've read many of Warren Buffett's annual reports. In every case, what fascinates me is that he is able to reduce things to the simplest of terms.

Many accomplished Wall Street gurus can make you dizzy with talk of intricate financial maneuverings. They might impress you with their sophisticated computerized trading results, their fifty percent returns from options on products that may not even exist yet. Fortunes are won and lost every day in these markets, but as far as I'm concerned, those folks would be just as successful if they ditched their hedge funds and put all their money on their favorite roulette number at the Trump Taj Mahal Casino in Atlantic City.

You paid good money for this book, and I know you're expecting sophisticated investment advice. The wisest thing I can tell you is to invest only in products you understand, with people you know you can trust. Sometimes the best investments are the ones you don't make.

Get a Prenuptial Agreement

I've said it before—I even wrote a chapter on the art of the prenup in one of my other books—but I'll say it again for anyone about to propose: A prenuptial agreement doesn't mean that you won't always love your spouse. It doesn't mean that you have doubts about the person's integrity or questions about the relationship. All it means is that you recognize that life, especially the parts involving love and business, can be complicated. People have a right to protect their assets. If you own your own business and you're facing a difficult divorce without having secured a prenuptial agreement, your negligence could jeopardize the livelihoods of your employees. I know plenty of women who are supporting their husbands, and this advice applies equally to both sexes.

If I hadn't signed a prenup, I would be writing this book from the perspective of somebody who lost big. We needed a bus to get Ivana's lawyers to court. It was a disaster, but I had a solid prenup, and it held up.

A friend of mine is married to a woman who stands only five-foot-two, but he's petrified of what she will do to him in court, all because he didn't get a prenup. Before he met this woman, he'd had four unsuccessful marriages, yet he told me, "Donald, I'm so in love with this woman that I don't need a prenuptial agreement." I didn't have the courage to tell him what I was thinking to myself: Loser!

A year later, the marriage was over and he was going through hell. When I saw him, he looked like a frightened puppy.

There's nothing wrong with common sense. Be like Thoreau and simplify.

Cut Out
the Middleman

Wayne Newton is a great friend of mine, and he made a lot of money over the years. Unfortunately, given terrible advice, he lost his money and was forced to declare bankruptcy. Meanwhile, his lawyers were eating him alive.

He called me and said, "Donald, I heard you owed $9.2 billion to a hundred banks in the early nineties and you never went bankrupt. How did you do it? Because I just can't seem to get out of this mess. My lawyers are making a fortune and the banks are impossible."

I asked Wayne how many banks were involved. He told me it was three. "You're lucky," I said. "I had ninety-nine banks and I made a point of becoming best friends with everybody at every bank. You have to do the same."

I gave him some more advice, which he has generously acknowledged in many interviews. I told him, "Wayne, you are a major celebrity. Have your secretary call the three banks and get the person who is really in charge, not the figurehead, and personally talk to all three people. Arrange a meeting with them, ideally a dinner with them and their families. Get to know them. At the end of this period of time, they'll like you. They'll be impressed by you because you are a celebrity. They may control a lot of money, but they don't control fame, and people are impressed by fame. Forget your lawyers. They are never going to want to settle the case, because then their legal fees stop. You must do it yourself. Call the bankers. Become friendly with the bankers. And make a deal."

Wayne called me three weeks later. He'd had dinner with all three bankers and said they were among the nicest people he'd ever met. They brought their wives and children. Later, he cut deals with every one of them. The banks were taken care of over a period of time, the lawyers didn't get any richer, and today Wayne is doing fantastically well.

You're probably wondering how this rule applies to your life if you are not headlining a major Las Vegas show. Here's how: Wayne took control of the situation. He appealed to the people in charge. Most of us need lawyers at some point in our lives, and we all have to deal with large bureaucracies. But sometimes you need to go right to the top, and you need to do it yourself. You don't have to sing "Danke Schoen" to make a sincere personal approach.

Of course, there will be times when lawyers are essential. Some people are scoundrels.* In those instances, sue the bastards. But whenever possible, settle. It saves a lot of time for everyone involved.

---

*I have come to hate doctors. I think that, generally, they are a bunch of money-grubbing dogs. I can tell you about countless instances when doctors have ruined people's lives. As an example, a person I am very fond of had a foot injury that I believe should have healed naturally, but instead, the doctor operated on it, fitting pins and plates into the foot. Now, after over a year of convalescence, this person is having a hard time walking. I think that suing a doctor like this would qualify as a worthwhile legal expense. (Recently, the patient saw this doctor walking on the very expensive and chic Worth Avenue in Palm Beach and spending lots of money.) This is one of many bad doctors I know of—there are too many others to name. I just can't stand the bastards.

Teach Your Children the Value of a Dollar

My kids know the value of money from example. They see how hard I work. I don't talk about it with them because I don't have to—they have eyes.

They see the way I live. I turn off the lights whenever I leave the office. I'm always happy to get a good deal, whether I'm buying a building or buying supplies at Duane Reade. (Trust me: You can get a good deal on shaving cream there.)

I always remember the example my parents set for me. I could *see* their determination and discipline. They didn't have to harp on it. I try to be the way they were.

My parents were frugal in the sense that they knew it wasn't easy to make money, and that it should be treated with respect. They lived well but simply, and were not flamboyant in their spending. We rarely went out to eat. We took relatively few elaborate vacations.

They emphasized schooling and education. We had a solid family life, and I remember feeling very fortunate. Each of us was expected to contribute something not only to the family as a whole, but to society. That is a Trump family value that is ingrained in me, and one I've tried to live up to.

*With my mother at
New York Military Academy.*

*With my father,
Fred Trump, in
the early days.*

My children have benefited from affluence, as I did, but it's surprising how unspoiled they are in many ways. They have budgets and live within them. They have limits on their credit cards, and they have them more for protection in an emergency than for anything else. When they were growing up, both of my sons earned extra money during their summer vacations by mowing lawns, cutting trees, moving stones, and doing landscaping work at the Seven Springs estate in Westchester. Ivanka attended the School of American Ballet, which requires an enormous amount of discipline and training.

College kids today are more money savvy, perhaps, than kids from earlier generations. They seem serious about their money. This is a good sign, because the sooner you understand the value of money, the more likely you are to possess large amounts of it.

If your children see you being careless with money, they will assume it's okay for them to be careless. Children watch. That's how they learn. Your priorities will often become their priorities. Any family can have a wild card or two, but on the whole, it's been proven that children will learn from what they see.

If you obviously enjoy going to Las Vegas to gamble, it's likely they'll think this is a good thing and will follow suit. If you like going to Carnegie Hall and bring the kids along, they'll think this is an exciting event because you do. Children inherently like to please, so think about the values you exhibit. Sooner or later, kids will form their own tastes, but the initial exposure is important.

I spent a good deal of time with my children—Don Jr., Ivanka, and Eric—when they were growing up, because we all lived together. We remain very close. I spend less time with Tiffany, as she lives in California with her mother. I do try to include them in my travels and activities as much as possible.

They know they are always welcome to join the family business. Don Jr. began working full-time at The Trump Organization in September 2001. "Trumps are builders," he told Barbara Walters in a

*With my three eldest children—
Don Jr., Ivanka, and Eric—
and Barbara Walters for an
appearance on 20/20.
(© 2004 Virginia Sherwood/ABC
Photo Archives)*

*With my youngest
daughter, Tiffany.*

recent interview. I hope Ivanka, Eric, and Tiffany might also consider a career with us, but it's their decision entirely.

I have very high standards, but so do my kids. They're all high achievers who enjoy working and are not goof-offs in any sense of the word. I wonder why I'm so lucky.

Not teaching your kids about money is like not caring whether they eat. If they enter the world without financial knowledge, they will have a much harder go of it. Make sure you let them in on your way of thinking about money—how you manage expenses, how you save, where you invest.

Let them know that having money isn't necessarily a sign of greed. It's an important element for survival. Just getting a first apartment can be a lesson for your kids: They suddenly learn about security deposits! Equip them for life as best you can. Buy them a subscription to *Money* or some other personal-finance magazine. Give them incentives for saving their allowance.

If they don't learn about money from you, who's going to teach them?

PART IV

The Secrets
of Negotiation

Negotiations, anyone? Here I am with George Foreman and Lennox Lewis.

If You Have Them
by the Balls,
Their Hearts and Minds
Will Follow

In this part of the book, I want to tell you about some of my favorite deals and the essential rules of negotiation they exemplify.

First, though, here's my basic philosophy of how deals are done: It's all about persuasion, not power.

Power is merely the ability to convince people to accept your ideas.

Just because I am a successful businessman doesn't mean I always get my way. It's true that I don't have to be as vociferous about things as before. I don't have to act like a bulldozer to get attention. But I have to coax and make my case just like any other negotiator.

An interviewer from Brazil recently asked me what the best parts and the worst parts of having so much money and success were. I had the same answer to both questions: the effect it has on people. Anyone in a position of power will probably agree with me. There are pluses and minuses.

The plus side is that people will listen to you more readily than if you aren't on the map financially. The minus side is that they will reduce you to one dimension and keep you there.

Power is not just about calling all the shots. It's about ability. You can call all the shots, but if they're bad ones, no one will take much notice after a while. *Know what you're doing.* That's where the real power comes from.

Convincing others has a lot to do with understanding negotiation. Study the art of persuasion. Practice it. Develop an understanding of its profound value across all aspects of life.

Don't expect people to believe your blarney simply because you're good at delivering it. The boardroom is not the pub down on the corner.

Make it easy on the people you are trying to convince. Give them readily accessible metaphors and analogies. If you are too far over their heads, they'll feel frustrated or, worse, inferior. Let them know you're all on the same level in some way. Use humor. It's a great icebreaker. I sometimes tell people that I wish our meeting had been yesterday, because I was having a great hair day and they missed it!

Convincing other people of how wonderful you are and how lofty your ideas are is a good way to convince them to tune out or, better yet, to escape from you as soon as possible. We all need to have a healthy dose of confidence to be convincing, but don't bulldoze. If you do, you may see a lot of people in front of you at first, but the room will soon be empty.

As the adage goes, "There's a fine line between acceptance and resignation." You want people to *accept* your ideas, not merely be *resigned* to them because they think they can't fight back or are just plain exhausted by you. Don't browbeat them into believing you. Let them think the decision is theirs. It will give them a feeling of control.

Here is the golden rule of negotiating:

He who has the gold makes the rules.

If you walk into a negotiation and know nothing about the other party, let *them* talk, listen to their tone, observe their body language, and determine whether they really want to make a deal or just show you how smart they are.

Most negotiations should proceed calmly, rather than in a hostile manner. However, sometimes a negotiation works best after a few screams and some table pounding.

The best negotiators are chameleons. Their attitude, demeanor, approach, and posture in a negotiation will depend on the person on the other side of the table.

If the other party to the transaction wants to acquire something you own, let them convince you that you really don't want it or need it. In doing so, they'll convince you of just how badly they want it.

Money is not always the only consideration for exchange in the sale of an asset. Think beyond the traditional boundaries.

Learn the value of saying no. View any conflict as an opportunity.

Most important, know the party on the other side of the table before sitting down with them. Research who you're dealing with, how they negotiate, and what they want from you.

Now you're ready to deal. The following stories illustrate these basic rules.

The Trump Building at 40 Wall Street.

Consider What
the Other Side Wants

One of the best deals I ever made was the acquisition of the tallest building in lower Manhattan, a 1.3-million-square-foot landmark known as 40 Wall Street.

I got it for $1 million, and the negotiation was all about timing and intuition.

In the 1960s and 1970s, 40 Wall Street was truly a hot property— a fully occupied building. Then in the 1980s, it was bought by Ferdinand Marcos, who was busy dealing with a revolution in the Philippines. The skyscraper at 40 Wall Street fell into decline, proving once again that a business should never be run by a dictator, especially a real one about to be booted from power.

Then the Resnicks, a prominent real estate family, descended on 40 Wall Street, but after a long period of negotiation, it became clear that the Resnicks and Citibank weren't going to make a deal and that 40 Wall Street would be back on the block. I wanted very much at this time to make my move, but this was in the early 1990s and I was in no position to do so. The real estate market was terrible, and my own financial straits were woeful.

The next buyer was the Kinson Company, a group from Hong

Kong. They made a great deal, and after the purchase was complete, I requested a meeting with them to discuss a possible partnership. They weren't interested in a partnership, but they did want to make 40 Wall Street the downtown equivalent of Trump Tower, including a public atrium. It sounded like a beautiful idea. However, what they would do with the steel columns that supported a seventy-two-story building never seemed to enter their minds. I was dumbfounded.

As you can probably guess, the Kinson group proved to be relatively clueless about renovating, running, and leasing out a New York City skyscraper. They weren't in the real estate business to begin with—they were mostly in apparel—and they were in way over their heads. They poured tens of millions of dollars into the building but were getting nowhere. They had problems with tenants, contractors, suppliers, architects, even the owners of the land, a prominent family from Germany, the Hinnebergs. Eventually, Kinson wanted out, and they called me.

It was now 1995 and the market still wasn't so good. Kinson had every reason to want to get out, and they wanted to do it quickly and quietly. So the negotiations began, with me offering them $1 million in addition to assuming and negotiating their liens. I also made the deal subject to a restructured ground lease with the Hinneberg family.

They accepted my terms without question.

Why? Because they wanted out—and fast. They knew it and I knew it, and because I knew it, the negotiation was easy.

There was another crucial aspect to this deal, which proves the importance of knowing what the other side wants: All of the prior leaseholders had dealt with the agent of the Hinneberg family. The agent insisted on increasing the rent and raised other financial obstacles that he said the owner insisted upon. I had to see for myself what the Hinnebergs wanted—was it money, or something else? If you want the truth, go to the source and skip the translation by the intermediary.

I flew to Germany with Bernie Diamond, my general counsel, for a face-to-face meeting with the owner, who seemed impressed by the fact that I would travel across the Atlantic to see him. I learned that what he really wanted was peace of mind in connection with his ownership of the land, but all he was getting was aggravation and litigation. I told him I would agree to turn the present disaster into a first-class office building if he would forgo all rent during the renovation period and revise the lease to permit rental to quality subtenants and bank financing for part of the building improvements. He agreed—and it was the first of many instances that confirmed my belief that Walter, Christian, and Walter Hinneberg Jr. are among the finest people with whom I've ever done business.

Very soon after acquiring 40 Wall Street, the markets turned for the better, and the downtown area experienced a renaissance in terms of both commercial and residential properties and developments.

I make a great deal of money from 40 Wall Street. Aside from owning the most beautiful building in lower Manhattan, I have the added attraction of owning a particularly lucrative one, all because I watched the property carefully for decades, waiting for my moment, and knew what the other side was thinking.

Be Reasonable and Flexible

A good negotiator must be flexible to be successful.

When I bought 40 Wall Street, it was virtually vacant. I told the existing leasing broker, a friend of mine, that I was going to renovate the building and get tenants. I offered him the chance to be my exclusive rental agent. The broker had been the agent for the previous owners of the building, who had been having big problems getting tenants. He was so sure I would fail that he said he would take the job only if I would pay him a retainer of $60,000 per month, starting immediately. He said he would deduct his future commission from that guaranteed fee.

His offer was impossible for me to accept. I owned a vacant building with existing losses, and the broker, who had been unable to produce in the past, was asking me to pay cash up front. I told the broker that his offer showed a total lack of faith in my ability to be successful—a broker getting paid without producing a tenant was unheard of.

The broker remained inflexible in his position. We parted company.

I hired another high-quality broker, who willingly accepted the opportunity on the usual terms—no lease, no commission. I renovated the building. The broker made millions in commissions in the next two years. The original broker's inflexibility cost him a small fortune, plus he lost any future business from me.

Trust Your Instincts

When I took over 40 Wall Street, my associate Abe Wallach, who orchestrated the purchase, was certain that the only viable solution was to convert the building to a residential cooperative apartment house. His reasoning made sense, given the depressed market for office tenants and the incentives the city was giving for residential development downtown. All of the real estate brokers shared his view that leasing to office tenants wasn't feasible. They said the floor sizes were either too small or too large for renting. They complained that the lobby, elevators, and building systems required extensive renovations with questionable results.

I was leery of their recommendation because the cost of residential conversion was high, plus the five floors occupied by a law firm would have to be bought out for megabucks and that would screw up any construction timetable. My instincts told me the building could become the prime office location it once had been, and that there had to be a way to make it work.

I asked George Ross to see whether he could devise a workable scenario, and he came up with an interesting new approach. He suggested we envision the 1.3-million-square-foot building as three separate structures on top of each other:

- The top 400,000-square-foot tower had small floors with spectacular views, and he was convinced it would quickly be rented to boutique tenants who would pay higher rent for the prestige of being a full-floor user on a high floor.
- The middle 300,000 square feet could be rented for less per square foot, but those rents would still more than cover the purchase price and the cost of renovation.
- The bottom 400,000 square feet might be tougher to rent, but even if those floors were completely empty, the building would still be profitable, assuming our projections about renting the top 700,000 square feet were correct.

Emboldened by George's plan, I discarded the idea of residential conversion and relied on our construction expertise to turn 40 Wall Street into a successful office building. We redesigned and modernized the lobby and building systems, and when the rental market improved, we were ready. Now, the building is worth hundreds of times what I paid for it.

I guess my instincts were right.

Know Exactly
What You Want
and Keep It to Yourself

If you're careful about what you reveal, you'll have more flexibility as you gather more information about the contours of the deal.

In order to complete Trump Tower as I envisioned it, it was necessary for me to control an adjoining site on Fifty-seventh Street owned by Leonard Kandell and leased to Bonwit Teller, a dying department store chain. Len Kandell was a shrewd real estate developer whose ultimate desire was to own land in strategic locations forever. I tried to gain a long-term lease, but Kandell was asking for too much in rent, and we were stalled.

Meanwhile, during negotiations to buy air rights from the adjoining Tiffany store, which would allow me to build a larger Trump Tower, I learned that Tiffany also had an option to buy the Kandell property at a fair market price. This was news to me, and a crucial piece of information, but I didn't let anyone know how important that news was to me.

I led Tiffany to believe I was interested only in air rights, without calling any special attention to their option to buy the Kandell property. They sold me their air rights and basically threw in the option as part of the deal.

Then I told Len Kandell that I was no longer interested in a lease on the land. I was going to buy it, using the Tiffany option.

Kandell didn't want to sell, and I really didn't want to buy. With my new leverage, I suggested reconsideration of a long-term lease. This time, Kandell agreed, and we quickly closed on a mutually acceptable lease, beginning a friendship that continues to flourish with his heirs.

Don't be confined by your expectations. Sometimes, what we think we want and what we actually want are two different things.

On more than several occasions, I have discovered in the middle of negotiations that what I had wanted was the wrong thing. Sometimes, my negotiating partners have given me ideas I hadn't thought of. Even adversaries have given me new ideas. Sometimes, a big question suddenly comes into my mind and I begin to think in a new direction.

Cut yourself some slack. It's okay to change your mind and suggest a different approach—as long as you haven't made any commitments to the other side.

Some people, while admitting I'm a good negotiator, have said I'm devious. I'm too busy to be devious. I just assimilate new information quickly and move forward in unexpected ways—unexpected to the other party as well as to myself. That's one reason I find negotiating exciting.

Perhaps because I'm a Gemini, I believe there is a duality to negotiating. You have to balance reason with passion. Reason keeps you open. Passion keeps your adrenaline going.

Before you begin any negotiation, write down your objectives. Then try to anticipate what the other side might want. Find a way of talking about the deal and setting up parameters that will keep either of you from getting locked into an impossible position.

Know what you want, bottom line, but keep it to yourself until a strategically necessary moment. Once all of the issues are on the table, you'll have a better approach to navigating your way to your desired solution.

Make Sure Both Sides Come Out Winning

In *The Art of the Deal,* I described how I acquired the Hilton property in Atlantic City, now known as Trump Marina, for $320 million. It was the biggest gamble of my career at the time, and it became front page news because the property was also sought by Steve Wynn, the largest casino owner in Las Vegas, who launched a hostile takeover bid before Hilton chose me as its white knight.

I like all of my Atlantic City hotels, but Trump Marina is where I prefer to stay when I'm in town, because acquiring this property was a victory to savor. It reminds me of an essential negotiating skill: Let everyone come out a winner. There was no rancor in this triumph.

There was drama, however—especially when Steve Wynn got involved. It became a competition of heavy hitters, and I loved every minute of it. I'll bet Steve did, too. To this day, we are good friends.

Interestingly enough, we are now both fodder for an HBO movie in development about Atlantic City. I got a copy of the script and it takes plenty of shots at me and Steve. It is highly inaccurate.

Steve, in essence, provided a catalyst for both the Hiltons and myself to get what we wanted. Was Steve the loser? No. I got the property I wanted, but Steve is thriving. The battle for the property enlarged his reputation and probably helped him move on to even bigger deals.

If the HBO movie ever makes it to the small screen, don't believe what you see. You'll get a better view of reality from other TV shows on the air. In a good negotiation, all sides win.

Let Your Guard Down, but Only on Purpose

Offer a calculated nugget of information, or a provocative opinion, to see what the reaction is.

If you say something seemingly off the cuff, you may get a revealing response. I might make an outrageous comment in a meeting just to see whether the other people play along or take a stand and disagree. It's a good way of assessing the mettle of the folks across the table. Do they want to be liked? Are they comfortable with unpredictability? Are they capable of candor?

Know that your negotiating partner might bluff, too. But when it comes to serious endeavors, you don't want bluffers of any sort. Study the person's history.

I'm always surprised when newcomers to the real estate industry think that talking big and fast will get them somewhere with me. Construction of a big building is painstaking work and that's the kind of person I want doing it—someone who will take the time to do it right. I don't want people who think they can get it done in record time. That can spell disaster.

I remember one contractor who tried every angle to convince me how fast he was. His time estimates were so far off that I couldn't take him seriously, but I let him keep trying to pitch me just to find out how full of it he really was. He must have thought he caught me on a bad day or with my guard down, but my guard wasn't down—I was just incredulous. Finally, I told the guy that what he was saying was exactly what I never wanted to hear. He was the first person whose bid was ruled out.

Being Stubborn
Is Often an Asset

My first big deal, in 1974, involved the old Commodore Hotel site near Grand Central Station on Forty-second Street in New York City. The hotel was vacant, except for a sleazy club called Plato's Retreat and some rundown street-level stores.

The land was owned by the Penn Central Railroad, which was bankrupt and owed New York City $15 million in back taxes that the city desperately needed. The city was about to default on its bonds, and banks would not consider real estate loans in Manhattan.

My idea was to transform the Commodore into a state-of-the-art hotel. I had a six-point plan:

1. Buy the land from the railroad.
2. Induce the railroad to use the purchase price to pay the City of New York the back taxes it owed.
3. Convince a New York State agency with the power of eminent domain to accept a deed to the land to condemn all existing leases.
4. Persuade the city to accept a fixed rental and a share of the profits in lieu of taxes.
5. Find a big hotel operator to join me in the project, since I had no hotel experience.
6. Convince a bank to loan me $80 million to build the hotel.

When I first told my lawyer, George Ross, of my plans, he told me I was crazy to attempt something so bold in such a bad economic environment. I told him I was determined to get it done. He agreed to help.

For two years, I stuck to my guns. Eventually, it paid off.

The railroad sold me the land for $12 million and used the money to pay the city its back taxes.

The Urban Development Corporation accepted the deed to the land and agreed to condemn all existing leases, provided I would pay all damages to the displaced tenants.

The city agreed to the lease from UDC with a fixed rent and a share of the profits.

Hyatt became my partner in the deal and funded half of it.

I got a loan from the Bowery Savings Bank to cover the cost of acquisition and construction.

The hotel became the Grand Hyatt.

The fact that I was stubborn and had achieved a result others deemed impossible jump-started my career as a developer.

Be Patient

I like to move quickly, but if a situation requires patience, I will be patient. The speed depends on the circumstances, and I keep my objective in mind at all times. This alone can be a patience pill. I've spent from five minutes to fifteen years waiting for a deal.

One good tactic for speeding up a deal is to show a lack of interest in it. This will often make the other side rekindle their efforts to get something going. I was very interested in a deal once, but I had a hunch that it wasn't a good idea to look too eager to these people. I would put off their calls and do my best to appear aloof. Then I said I'd be traveling for a couple of weeks and would get back to them after that. While I was "traveling," they used the time to modify their position and present to me almost precisely what I'd been hoping to get. It saved us all a lot of negotiating time.

A good tactic for slowing down a deal is to distract the other side. One way is to drop hints about whether a certain aspect of the deal should be looked into further, or to mention other deals and properties as examples. That will set them off in a direction that consumes their time and focus. While they're off on a tangent, you'll still be on target.

One time, I was in the middle of a negotiation that seemed to be speeding out of my control. I suddenly asked the other side if they knew the history of a particular development, implying that their understanding of it might be crucial. They figured the development must have had some bearing on what we were trying to accomplish together, so they backed up a bit, took some time to investigate it, and gave me control of the negotiations with enough time to assess everything at my leisure. I got the upper hand.

Life at the top means the phone calls never stop.

Be Strategically Dramatic

In 1999, I began construction on the tallest residential tower in the world, Trump World Tower at the United Nations Plaza.

The location was terrific—the East Side of Manhattan, close to the United Nations, with both river views and city views. It was hot stuff, but not everyone was happy about it, especially some diplomats at the United Nations, who didn't want their thirty-eight-story building to be outclassed by our ninety-story tower. According to CNN, UN secretary general Kofi Annan acknowledged talking with New York City mayor Rudolph Giuliani about the project and how to stop it.

"It will not fit here," the Ukrainian ambassador, Volodymyr Yel'chenko, told CNN, "because it overshadows the United Nations complex."

When the protests became vocal, I used my own brand of diplomacy and refused to say anything critical of the United Nations. I predicted that many ambassadors and UN officials would end up buying apartments in the building. Sure enough, they have.

But as soon as we were in business, the city hit us with an enormous tax assessment, costing us over $100 million more than we thought we should pay. We decided to take the only action possible.

We sued the city for $500 million.

For four years, we fought this case. The city lawyers held their ground, and we held ours. We could have given up. It's not easy to take on the government and win, especially when the issue is taxes, but I knew we had a case.

Finally, after many conversations, we reached a settlement. The city agreed to cut our taxes seventeen percent and give us the ten-year tax abatement that we sought if we would agree to withdraw our lawsuit and subsidize two hundred units of affordable housing in the Bronx.

The lawsuit saved us approximately $97 million. We never would have gotten any of it if we hadn't taken dramatic action.

Sometimes
You Still
Have to Screw Them

For many years I've said that if someone screws you, screw them back. I once made the mistake of saying that in front of a group of twenty priests who were in a larger audience of two thousand people. I took some heat for that. One of them said, "My son, we thought you were a much nicer person."

I responded, "Father, I have great respect for you. You'll get to heaven. I probably won't, but to be honest, as long as we're on the earth, I really have to live by my principles."

When somebody hurts you, just go after them as viciously and as violently as you can. Like it says in the Bible, an eye for an eye.

Be paranoid. I know this observation doesn't make any of us sound very good, but let's face the fact that it's possible that even your best friend wants to steal your spouse and your money. As I say every week in *The Apprentice*, it's a jungle out there. We're worse than lions—at least they do it for food. We do it for the thrill of the hunt.

Recently, I've become a bit more mellow about retribution and paranoia. Although I still believe both are necessary, I now realize that vengeance can waste a lot of time better spent on new developments and deals, and even on building a better personal life. If you can easily dismiss a negative from your life, it's better to do so. Seeing creeps as a form of corruption that you're better off without is a great time-saving device.

Still, sometimes you've just got to screw them back.

For example, a while ago I agreed to invest a small amount in a new restaurant venture. I did this with the full expectation that I was throwing this money down the drain, because most of these clubs are not successful. I liked the two young guys who approached me to invest and figured I'd give them a break—plus a good friend of mine had asked me to help them.

When the restaurant opened, it was a smash hit. Crowds of people lined up to get in. Money was pouring in. It was incredible.

About a year later, I realized that I hadn't received a single dollar from the owners—no repayment of my initial investment and certainly no profit. I called two of the guys who got me into the deal and said, "Fellas, come on, I know success when I see it. You ought to pay back your investors."

One of them said, "Oh, we're working so hard, and the money just isn't coming in fast enough."

My response: "Bullshit! I don't believe it." From my perspective, they seemed to be living like kings.

Eventually, I received my first "equity distribution" from them, for a fraction of my investment. I was furious and sent an angry letter to the managing partner, in which I asked for a public investigation of their records.

I'm an instinctive businessman and I hate being screwed. I can't prove they did anything wrong without spending more money to investigate them than my investment is worth, but my hunch is that investors like me should have been repaid six times their initial investment by now.

Now whenever I see the guys I tried to help, they wave to me and I just turn my back. The sad thing for them is that had I felt that they treated me (and their other investors) fairly, I probably would have backed them for millions on their next deal.

Maybe I'll sue them anyway, just to prove my point. Business can be tough, but you've got to stay true to your principles.

Sometimes
You Have to
Hold a Grudge

For years, I supported the governor of New York Mario Cuomo. I was one of his largest campaign contributors. I never asked for a thing while he was in office. For my generous support, he regularly thanked me and other major contributors with a tax on real estate so onerous that it drove many investors away from the city. It became known as the Cuomo Tax.

After he was defeated for reelection by a better man (and governor), George Pataki, I called Mario to ask for a perfectly legal and appropriate favor involving attention to a detail at the Department of Housing and Urban Development, which at the time was being run by his son Andrew.

Mario told me that this would be hard for him to do, because he rarely calls the "Secretary" on business matters.

I said to him, "Mario, he is not the Secretary. He's your son."

Mario said, "Well, I think of him as the Secretary, and I refer to him as that—he's got a very serious job to do."

I understood Mario's concern about impropriety, but I wasn't asking him to do anything even slightly questionable—this was a simple, aboveboard request, the kind of favor that takes place between friends in the private and public sectors all the time. Finally, I asked Mario point-blank, "Well, are you going to help me?"

In a very nice way, he essentially told me no.

I did the only thing that felt right to me. I began screaming. "You son of a bitch! For years I've helped you and never asked for a thing, and when I finally need something, and a totally proper thing at that, you aren't there for me. You're no good. You're one of the most disloyal people I've known and as far as I'm concerned, you can go to hell."

My screaming was so loud that two or three people came in from adjoining offices and asked who I was screaming at. I told them it was Mario Cuomo, a total stiff, a lousy governor, and a disloyal former friend. Now whenever I see Mario at a dinner, I refuse to acknowledge him, talk to him, or even look at him.

I will say this, however. Mario's wife, Matilda, is a fine woman and was a terrific friend to my mother. It's not her fault that her husband is a loser.

Another failed politician who disappointed me is a man named Pete Dawkins, sometimes referred to as General Pete Dawkins. He led a charmed life—West Point cadet, Heisman trophy winner, Rhodes scholar, but as I found out, Pete was also a stiff. When he was running for the U.S. Senate in New Jersey against Frank Lautenberg, a magazine called *Manhattan, Inc.* published a damning profile of him, and Dawkins folded up like a broken umbrella.

One day, Dawkins came to my office and asked me to help him build the Vietnam Veterans Memorial in lower Manhattan. He asked for a million dollars (or more) because he said he was having bad luck raising money.

I decided to help because no soldiers have ever been treated worse than the courageous people who came back from Vietnam, wounded and maimed, attacked physically abroad and psychologically at home.

I provided over a million dollars in matching grants, and, almost as important, I helped get it built by using the best contractors in the city, along with unions who made sure it was constructed swiftly, properly, and cost-effectively. At the opening, Pete Dawkins took the credit.

Many years later, he was working as a high-ranking executive at Citibank and I phoned him to ask a small favor, to find something out for me. He didn't respond for a while, so I called him two more times. Finally, he said, "I really can't do it for you, Donald, and I really don't want to get involved." I told Dawkins that the *Manhattan, Inc.* article about him had been true. I consider him to be one of the most over-rated people I have ever dealt with.

Sometimes you have to hold a grudge.

The hugely successful Miss Universe Pageant. From left to right: Charles Gargano, Stephanie Seymour, Evander Holyfield, Miss Universe Wendy Fitzwilliams, me, and NFL great Bruce Smith. Also pictured: Kylie Bax (third from right) and Sirio Maccioni (far right).

Learn the Value
of Saying No

I purchased the Miss Universe Organization in 1996 and immediately sold half of the company to CBS; so not only were they our broadcaster, they were a co-owner as well. This kind of arrangement, where the network actually owns the end product, was a fairly new concept and should have been a win-win situation, since CBS would actually be able to eliminate the middleman and pay a lower license fee while, in theory, the network, as an owner, would look to maximize all promotional opportunities.

The partnership was a great concept, but after five years, it had not gone as planned. CBS was not willing to promote the shows to my satisfaction. As more and more cable competition ate into the network's market share, on-air promotion became all the more important to sustain viewership, but it just wasn't happening. To make matters worse, CBS tried to change the shows drastically by making them MTV-style music specials and dramatically cutting the time allotted to show the women competing. I am not a network programmer, but it seemed to me that people might be tuning in to a beauty competition to see beautiful women.

I am not saying a television musical performance is a bad thing;

there have been some great ones over the years. A perfect example was the 1999 Miss Teen USA pageant: A year earlier, the teen show had introduced a little-known boy band called 'NSync. By 1999 they were the biggest band around. As a sign of appreciation, they agreed to appear on the Miss Teen USA pageant again. In the middle of their summer tour, 'NSync rented a jet and flew in for eight hours the day of the show, performing two songs. They were terrific. Unfortunately, no one knew about it because CBS had chosen not to run a single promotion for the show.

So in February 2002 we were all reevaluating how we wanted to approach the network license renewal. Citing the current ratings, which were caused by the lack of promotion and the fact that CBS would always air the pageant against the toughest competition, Les Moonves, the head of the network, said he was not willing to begin negotiations until the end of the season. Obviously, with the season ending in August, the network schedules would be set and there would be absolutely no room for negotiation with any other network.

I sent a letter to Les telling him I wanted an option to buy CBS out of the partnership, exercisable up until a week after the broadcast of the Miss Universe pageant in May. I feigned disinterest in continuing with the pageants and told him if I did not exercise the option, we would commence with selling or dismantling the company. A few days later, I believed we had a deal.

I immediately signed with Jim Griffin of the William Morris Agency to begin shopping the pageants to other broadcasters. I also called my good friend Bob Wright, chairman and CEO of NBC, to tell him the pageants might become available. I knew that NBC had recently acquired Telemundo, and the pageants are huge in Latin markets. It looked like a great opportunity for cross-promotion.

In the meantime, CBS had given up and allowed us free rein to get back to the basics on the production and put more emphasis on what had worked in the past: beautiful women. We also convinced them to schedule the pageant for a night outside of the all-important ratings sweeps, which would ensure more on-air promotions.

As a result, our 2002 Miss Universe pageant hit ratings gold. Overall, it was number seven for the week and number one in demographics. The pageant even trounced the NBA playoffs on NBC. The Miss Universe pageant quickly became a very hot property.

I immediately sent a letter to Les Moonves telling him I was exercising my option to buy out CBS. To my shock, Les took the position that we had never agreed on an option. NBC was waiting in the wings, and after a weeklong bidding war I bought out CBS and created a new partnership with NBC.

At the first meeting of the new board, I asked the Miss Universe staff to dust off some of the cross-promotional ideas they had pitched to CBS over the years. Within minutes, Jeff Gaspin of NBC approved the production of a Miss USA *Fear Factor* to lead into the Miss USA telecast. In addition, the *Today* show agreed to do five-minute live shots from each pageant location. The results were amazing. For years the pageants had tried to get a plug on the third-rated *CBS Morning Show* and couldn't get as much as a returned phone call. Now they were getting major promotion on the nation's number one morning program and an Internet tie-in through NBC.com.

The Miss USA *Fear Factor* was the highest rated in the series and the 2003 Miss USA and Miss Universe pageants received the highest ratings since I had bought the company. Additionally, the Telemundo simulcast of the pageant was one of the highest-rated programs in the network's history.

The cross-promotional concept I visualized in 1996 was finally realized in 2003, and it never would have happened if I hadn't been willing to walk away from CBS, say no, and pursue a better opportunity elsewhere.

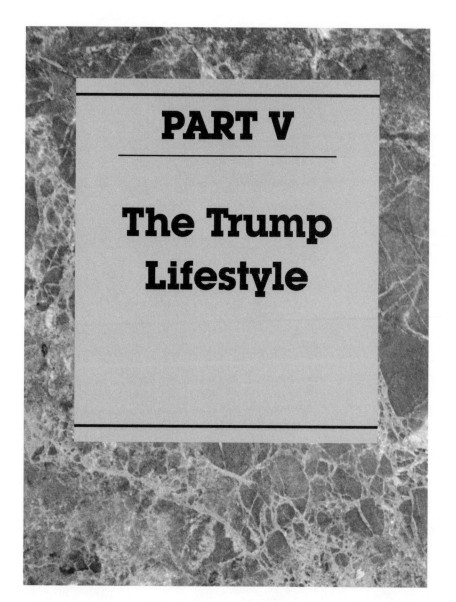

PART V

The Trump Lifestyle

The art of the hair.

The Art of the Hair

Over the years, I have been criticized for the way I comb my hair, but never so much as since the opening show of *The Apprentice*. *New York* magazine wrote that I'd "perfected the pompad-over." *The New York Times* called it "an elaborate structure best left to an architecture critic."

David Letterman and Jay Leno regularly do quips about it. Matt Lauer, who with Katie Couric has taken the *Today* show to new heights, told me I should just give up the ghost and shave it off or give myself some kind of buzz cut like the one he has. Likewise, Pat O'Brien, the star of *Access Hollywood*, told me he had heard about Matt Lauer's comment and totally agrees with him.

Personally, I think it looks good, but I've never said my hair was my strongest point. I told Pat and Matt that I'm just not ready to change my style. I've been combing it this way for a long time and I might as well keep doing it. The ratings of *The Apprentice* are sky-high, and maybe they would drop if I changed the look at this point.

I'm amazed by how often people ask me whether or not I wear a hairpiece, a wig, or a rug, as it is affectionately known.

The answer, for the record, is emphatically and categorically no: I do not wear a rug. My hair is one hundred percent mine. No animals have been harmed in the creation of my hairstyle.

However, I must admit that the day may come when I will wear a hairpiece, wig, or rug—but only if I go bald, which I hope never happens. The reason for this is because I, like most men, am very vain. Many times over the years, I've heard people say that men are vainer than women, and I believe it. Guys don't like to talk about it, but Random House is paying me a fortune for this book and specifically requested a chapter on "the art of the hair," so I will admit to my vanity.

I will also reveal some of my hair-related secrets.

The reason my hair looks so neat all the time is because I don't have to deal with the elements very often. I live in the building where I work. I take an elevator from my bedroom to my office. The rest of the time, I'm either in my stretch limousine, my private jet, my helicopter, or my private club in Palm Beach, Florida. If Matt Lauer had my lifestyle, he might not have changed his hairstyle—although his hair looks great now.

If I happen to be outside, I'm probably on one of my golf courses, where I protect my hair from overexposure by wearing a golf hat. It's also a way to avoid the paparazzi. Plus the hat always has a big TRUMP logo on it—it's an automatic promotion.

I will also admit that I color my hair. Somehow, the color never looks great, but what the hell, I just don't like gray hair.

I wonder how much longer my hair will be a national topic of conversation. Letterman and Leno have been funny, but one person I don't like is Joy Behar, a woman who works for Barbara Walters on *The View*. For weeks, she was attacking me, insisting that I wear a wig, so Barbara and her staff called me and asked if I would surprise them and appear on the show. I did, and when I ran my hand through my hair and proved that it was real, everybody laughed and that was the end of that.

After *The Apprentice* premiered, Joy Behar was on *The Tonight Show* along with the rest of the cast of *The View*. Out of the blue, Jay Leno started talking about the great success of *The Apprentice*. Star

Jones raved about it, as did the others—except for Joy Behar, a woman with no talent and a terrible accent, who again attacked my hair. I've always said that show would do better without her. I did her a favor by going on the show, and it was not appreciated. Being nice to some people never pays off.

I suppose it's possible that I could rethink my look for the second season of *The Apprentice*. But probably not—it seems to be working!

Gossip

Whether you're building a luxury apartment or producing a beauty pageant, you've got to give the people what they want.

In a book like this one, that means some good advice, some wisdom, a little bit of gossip, and a glimmer of fame.

I've done my best to give you some wisdom and advice. Now, here's a Palm Beach morality tale about gossip and fame:

I had a friend who was rich and successful and very married. For months, I kept hearing a rumor that he was having an affair with an equally successful businesswoman who was also very married. It was hard to believe. She was drop-dead gorgeous and could probably have had any guy she wanted. My friend was not a likely choice.

The rumors persisted, and then one day my friend invited me out to dinner with the gorgeous woman and her husband. I told him the invitation seemed strange to me. "For a long time, I've been hearing you're having an affair with her. Wouldn't you find it a little uncomfortable having dinner with her in front of her husband?"

Surprisingly, my friend confirmed that he was having the affair, that the woman's husband didn't know, and that he (my friend) was totally in love, something which he felt his wife, who was as tough as nails, would not exactly appreciate or understand.

Without revealing any of my friend's secrets, I told my girlfriend, Melania, to prepare for a wild evening.

We had dinner at a restaurant. Normally, I would have been watching the scene with great amusement, but the businesswoman's husband was also a friend of mine, and so I was in a precarious position. There we all sat, as though nothing was happening, but we could all feel tension in the air. As we left, I watched my friend grab the businesswoman around the waist in a more than familiar fashion. Her husband was out of sight when this happened, but it was clear to me that, despite my disbelief and amazement, there was something going on between the two.

Over the next few weeks, my friend called me incessantly, proclaiming his love for the woman. He said he would do anything to be with her, and that she was also in love with him. His calls became so frequent that Melania asked, "Why does he keep calling you? What's going on?" When I told Melania about the affair, she also found it hard to believe. As I said, this businesswoman is an amazing beauty and my friend is not exactly Brad Pitt—although he is very rich and some women find him handsome.

Finally, after a number of phone calls, I said, "Look, are you bullshitting me or is this for real?"

He said, "It is! It is! I want to come over and see you and I'll prove it." He didn't have to prove anything to me. What difference did it make? But I invited him over anyway.

When he arrived, he told me how they'd met, how the relationship was going, all the sordid details. I still wasn't sure I believed him, but then he played an answering machine tape of a call she had made to him. She said the kind of intimate things only a lover would say. It was truly down and dirty, and I definitely recognized her voice. There was no longer any doubt in my mind about what was taking place.

For a while, my friend continued to call me to say how much he loved this woman. If I was in Palm Beach when he called me, I would just watch the television and politely listen to what he was saying. I felt more like his psychiatrist than anything else.

Then the shit hit the fan! The woman's husband had found out, phoned my friend, and threatened to kill him. But what really bothered my friend was the next call he received—from the woman, saying she would never see him or talk to him again, and that if she did, her husband would tell my friend's wife everything about the affair. My friend was devastated. Afterward, he repeatedly tried to reach his ex-lover, but she refused to respond.

As usually happens, my friend's wife found out. Probably, the businesswoman's husband had called her, but who knows?

About six months later, I saw the businesswoman at a gallery and she confronted me. "Donald," she said, "I hear you've been spreading rumors all over town about me. It's terrible what you've done, and the rumors about me and [X] aren't true. Can you imagine me going out with him?" After listening to her accusations and denials for fifteen minutes, I realized she is one of the greatest salespeople I have ever known, because if I had not heard her voice on that answering machine tape, I would have completely believed her. She told me she couldn't believe people would even think she would go out with my friend. "Why would I want to? What did he have? Give me a break!"

I figured that was the end of it, but then I realized that my friend had not called me in some time. I was wondering how he was doing, so I phoned him to say hello. He wasn't in and didn't return my call. I phoned again, and again he didn't call back. I was worried, so I called a third time and a fourth time. No response.

Later, I found out that his wife had blamed me for the entire affair. She thought I had introduced him to this woman. Apparently, she told him that if he ever spoke to me again, she would divorce him.

It turns out he had used me as a scapegoat. The funny thing is, I wouldn't have minded and would have helped him out and played along if he'd had the decency, as a good friend, to call me and say,

"Look, I have a problem. Can I blame it on you?" Even if it meant he wouldn't have been able to see me or speak to me again, I would have accepted it and been glad to have helped keep his marriage together. But he never made that call to me. He did everything without an explanation.

Now when I see him at a restaurant or an event, nothing is said. But he knows, and I know.

I heard he was still suffering through his marriage. As a means of reconciliation, he bought his wife some tremendous jewelry. Apparently, she made him return it because it wasn't big enough or expensive enough. He had to go back and buy her something even bigger and better.

Page Six, My Way

The *New York Post* is a popular daily newspaper in this city. I read it every day, as do lots of other people. It contains a two-page spread called Page Six, which is not located on page six but is a must-read. Over the years it's been edited by a highly talented guy named Richard Johnson. He's got insight into everything, and he knows more about what's going on in New York than anyone I know. For better or for worse, I make Page Six a lot. I hope the day never comes when they don't find me interesting enough to mention. Meanwhile, here's my version of Page Six for my readers, so you'll be up on the latest.

I'm sure a lot of you have heard of **Ivana,** my first wife, who christened me "The Donald" and launched a thousand missiles—I mean smiles—in my direction. Well, I'm happy to report that she's doing well and at this moment is in the south of France, having, I hope, a great time. We are on good terms and speak often. We are still neighbors in New York City, and with three incredible children to share, we consider ourselves to be very fortunate people and good friends.

Marla, my second wife, is living in Los Angeles and is as beautiful as ever. Our daughter, Tiffany, is now ten years old, and continues to charm everything and everyone in sight. I don't see her as much as I'd like, but every minute is worth a bundle when I do.

With Richard Johnson of Page Six fame.

With the exquisite Melania Knauss.

I've spent the last five years with the exquisite **Melania Knauss,** a model from Slovenia. Anyone who has ever met her will never forget it. She's just as beautiful on the inside as she is on the outside. Despite her great beauty, she is a very calm and soothing person who has brought a sense of stability to my very turbulent life. I am lucky to be with her!

My eldest son, **Don Jr.,** joined The Trump Organization in September 2001 and has already proven himself to be a valuable member of our team. He, like me, graduated from the Wharton School at the University of Pennsylvania, and has since decided to join the family business and see what he can learn from his father. He's a good guy and will be a successful one, too.

Ivanka, my eldest daughter, is currently attending the Wharton School. She has already had a successful modeling career and is a heartbreaker in every way. She will do well no matter what she does.

Eric, my youngest son, is at Georgetown University and doing well. We have great expectations for him, and since he's already six feet six inches tall, that shouldn't prove to be a problem. He, like Don Jr., is an avid outdoorsman.

I remain very close to my brother **Robert** and to my sisters, **Maryanne** and **Elizabeth.** All are thriving, successful, and productive.

My parents, **Fred** and **Mary,** passed away in 1999 and 2000, respectively. The void they left will never be filled. But what each gave to me, by way of example, will remain with me every day of my life.

I love my family. They are very much my motivation. They always have been, and they always will be. Am I a rich man? Yes, very rich.

I also feel blessed to have some terrific friends and business associates.

Barbara Corcoran is a wonderful woman who did a tremendous job in creating the Corcoran Group. She then sold it for a substantial profit and has done well ever since. I will never be surprised by how well she does. A friend of mine recently sent me an article about Bar-

*With my daughter Ivanka and my son Eric
at Georgetown University.*

With Don Jr. and Eric at the Mar-a-Lago Club in Palm Beach, Florida.

bara in which she was asked about my influence on the residential market. She said, "Donald Trump has had singularly the greatest possible influence on Manhattan luxury real estate, simply because it was his marketing chutzpah that changed the perception of living in Manhattan." It's always nice to be complimented by pros, and Barbara is a total pro.

Another good friend is **Mohamed Al Fayed,** chairman of Harrods in Knightsbridge, London. Mohamed has gone through quite a rough time over the last several years—it was his son Dodie who was dating Princess Diana. To many of us, it looked like they would be getting married at some point in the not-too-distant future, until their lives ended in that tragic car crash in Paris. Mohamed is an extremely loyal father who has fought so hard for his son and the memory of him. I wish people understood him better. He is a truly good man.

Jack Welch is a particular favorite of mine. Now he's writing a book, and I'm going to be the first on line to buy it. Few people, if any, have ever done a better job of running a corporation.

I always enjoy being with **George Steinbrenner.** Quite honestly, there's no one like him, and he hasn't been appreciated to the extent he should be. I remember the Yankees when they couldn't win a game, when nobody went to Yankee Stadium, and the team was a total disaster. George puts a championship team on the field every year and does what it takes to win, whether people like him for it or not.

When we were taping *The Apprentice,* I told NBC that I would love to get George to give the candidates a lecture on winning. They looked at me and thought I was crazy, because the scene had to be shot that day and the World Series was beginning the following day. Knowing what a good friend George was, I was sure he would do it, and when I called him at Yankee Stadium he immediately picked up the phone and agreed. We were at Yankee Stadium thirty minutes later, and even the top people at NBC were impressed. The kids walked into this legendary office with its pictures of Babe Ruth, Joe DiMaggio, Mickey Mantle, and many other Yankee greats on the walls, and their eyes were wide open, as though they'd never seen anything like it before. George was incredibly nice. He sat with the kids for a long time, until I finally had to be the one to say, "George, you're busy as hell—let me get them out of here." He's really a great guy. People will appreciate George Steinbrenner only when they no longer have him, and when the Yankees are wallowing in last place.

Another sports owner who is one of the great winners is **Bob Kraft,** who helped lead the New England Patriots to a second Super Bowl victory. I've gotten to know Bob over the last two years, and there is no finer gentleman. He and his wife, Myra, are totally un-assuming. With his sons, Bob has methodically and brilliantly built a strong franchise in New England that was a total disaster before Kraft's ascent. **Tom Brady** is the best quarterback in football. There are other quarterbacks with impressive stats, but when you need someone to throw four or five completions in the final minutes of a game, there is nobody better than Tom. With all of their upcoming draft choices and the great players they already have, this team is only going to get bet-ter over the next few years.

Two other terrific team owners are **Jerry Jones,** owner of the Dal-las Cowboys, and **Bob Tisch,** owner of the New York Giants. Tisch has done so well in every capacity, whether it's business or sports. He's in his seventies, but he's got the attitude of someone in his twenties, thir-ties, or forties.

Larry Silverstein, the developer of the new World Trade Center complex, is a good friend of mine, but I really hate what's being designed for the site. It resembles a skeleton, and I can't believe Larry really wanted to evoke that image. In actuality, Larry is being forced to do certain things that he would not do under normal circum-stances, but he has to go with the flow. Nevertheless, I'm sure he'll do a terrific job.

Finally, since Page Six often takes a few digs at people, here are mine:

Dan Rather is not one of my favorite people. A few years ago, he wanted to profile me for *60 Minutes*. As we toured Mar-a-Lago and Trump International Golf Club in Florida, he couldn't have been nicer or more respectful. I was sure the interview would be a total home run.

When the interview aired, it couldn't have been nastier. He showed me giving a speech to an empty room at a poorly planned event, when the day before I'd given the same speech to a standing-room-only crowd. But *60 Minutes* didn't air that speech. They just wanted me to look as bad as possible.

Dan Rather is an enigma to me. He's got absolutely no talent or charisma or personality, yet year after year, CBS apologizes for his terrible ratings. I could take the average guy on the street and have him read the news on CBS and that guy would draw bigger ratings than Dan Rather does. When I see Rather at Yankee games, I stay away from him. However, I will say one nice thing about him: Recently, he was the emcee at a Police Athletic League dinner for District Attorney Robert Morgenthau, one of the great men in the history of New York City. Dan called me and told me he felt very uncomfortable being the emcee of a dinner for which I was the chairman. I told him I appreciated the call and that it would be fine with me if he was the emcee. He did a nice job, but I'll never forget what he did to me on *60 Minutes*. People don't change their stripes.

I'll conclude this with a story about **Howard Cosell,** a spectacular sportscaster who I got to know during the last ten years of his life. People either loved Howard or hated him—there was no in between—but he was really the best at what he did. As Howard grew older, though, he became nastier, even toward the people who loved him and had helped make him a success. He always felt that being a sportscaster was beneath him. He longed to run for the U.S. Senate.

Howard could sit on a dais with sports figures he hadn't seen for thirty years and quote their exact statistics. His memory was amazing.

Then he wrote his final book and knocked almost everyone he knew, from Roone Arledge to Frank Gifford, one of the finest people around. It did a lot of damage to him, because all of his friends turned against him. I remember saying to him, "Howard, you can knock twenty percent of the people, maybe twenty-five percent or thirty percent of the people, but you can't knock everybody. You didn't say anything nice about anybody in the book. It was the wrong thing to do. I believe in knocking people, but you can't knock everybody."

That's a rule I try to follow, in this book and in my life.

A Week in the Life

In *The Art of the Deal* and in my other two memoirs, I included a chapter about a typical week in my life. When I met Mark Burnett, the creator of *The Apprentice,* he told me it was his favorite chapter in the book, and a lot of other readers have told me the same thing. So, back by popular demand, here's an example of what an average eventful week was like in the fall of 2003.

This chapter doesn't have any specific advice on how to get rich, but it will show you how I have fun, and I doubt I'd be as successful as I am if I weren't having such a good time.

MONDAY

9:00 A.M. I have a meeting with architect Costas Kondylis, an elegant way to start the week. Costas and I have worked on several very successful projects together, including the Trump World Tower at the United Nations Plaza, Trump Park Avenue (at Fifty-ninth Street and Park Avenue, just completed), and, together with Philip Johnson and Skidmore Owings and Merrill, Trump Place, my sixteen-building development along the Hudson River. Some of you might remember that site as the West Side yards, which I have been involved with since

1974, when I first secured the option to purchase them from the Penn Central Railroad. That was my first major deal in Manhattan. Close to thirty years later, here we are discussing the fifth and sixth buildings under construction. (Never give up.)

My eldest son, Don Jr., is also at the meeting. We are on schedule with construction, and the first three condominium buildings have proven to be very successful. However, neither Costas nor myself is likely to ever rest on his laurels, and we are troubleshooting, going over every detail. If Costas hadn't been an architect, he'd have made a very good surgeon—he's just that meticulous. We get along famously, and I'd put him up there with Philip Johnson as one of our most outstanding architects.

We are also discussing the reaction to the city park I developed and donated to the city, which is on the West Side yards property. I hate to disappoint people, but my detractors were not pleased about this twenty-five-acre gift. What can I say? Except that you can't be all things to all people, no matter how hard you try.

I look over some kitchen and bathroom fixtures, and we decide to go with the top of the line. My name and work have become synonymous with quality, and there's a reason for it. We don't skimp on anything, ever or anywhere. Don Jr. mentions looking forward to the topping-out party for Building #4. That's a big day for builders, and it's a celebration when the frame of the building, the superstructure, is completed, and everyone involved meets at the top for a party.

9:30 A.M. Norma comes in to tell me that Oscar de la Renta is on the line, and Costas and I decide to meet again in a couple of weeks. Our new Miss Universe, Amelia Vega, is from Santo Domingo, which is also the birthplace of Oscar de la Renta. He wants to meet her, and I don't blame him. She's a beauty, all six feet of her. We're proud not only of her, but of the Miss Universe contest, which has become extremely successful since I bought it seven years ago. We beat out the competition in television ratings and we are highly regarded internationally as well. Ecuador has paid millions of dollars to host the 2004 contest, and we're looking forward to a great time there.

Back to Oscar—he's a class act all the way. His impeccable work speaks for itself.

9:45 A.M. I make a call to some wiseguy contractors who've been trying to cheat me. This can be a crummy business because of the scum of the earth it attracts, but you have to do what you have to do. Screaming at them is what I have to do.

10:00 A.M. I have three calls waiting: Mark Brown, the CEO and president of my three casinos in Atlantic City; Woody Allen's office; and Mayor Bloomberg. I take the mayor's call first, much as I respect Woody Allen and Mark. I think the mayor is doing a great job, considering he's got one of the toughest jobs on the planet. Running a corporation is one thing; running a city is another, especially this one.

Woody Allen may go down to Florida and stay at the Mar-a-Lago, my club in Palm Beach. I've been in one Woody Allen film, and I never miss any of his movies.

10:30 A.M. I have my first Diet Coke of the day. I know I should drink mineral water, and I do sometimes, but I really like Diet Coke. Irina Dvorovenko calls in; she's a ballerina at the American Ballet Theatre. She's not only a sensational dancer, but also an incredibly beautiful woman. I'm not exactly a ballet fan, but because of Irina, that might be a possibility.

Our wonderful mayor, Mike Bloomberg.

With another great mayor of New York City, Rudy Giuliani, in 2000.

The television crew from Neal Cavuto's team is ready for an interview. I ask what it's about, and then we're ready to go. After decades of interviews, they are easy for me to do, especially with someone like Neal, who is not only personable but also very knowledgeable. He and his team are pros all the way. And he gets the best business ratings on cable TV.

11:00 A.M. I received seventeen calls during the interview, and I begin to return them, in between the incoming calls. After so many years in business, knowing how to prioritize is second nature. It's also a key factor in keeping up your momentum, even during a typical workday, which is crucial if you intend to become or remain successful. Everyone's heard of the New York minute, but by now that's outdated—it's become the New York second. That's no exaggeration. Seconds count when you have hundreds of phone calls a day to handle. One bogged-down conversation, and your momentum could be interrupted for an hour. So when I say momentum is crucial, I mean it. You'll know when you've got it, and you'll know when it's being disrupted.

I return Joe Cinque's call; he's an executive with the American Academy of Hospitality Sciences, which presents the coveted Five Star Diamond award. My properties have received several of them. Joe is a high-spirited and generous man, but he's difficult to please and discerning when it comes to giving out awards. He's just returned from Sardinia and mentions that he still thinks the Mar-a-Lago Club in Palm Beach is the most beautiful resort he's ever seen, worldwide. Coming from him, that's saying something. I always liked Joe, and now I like him even more.

I return Regis Philbin's call. He and his wife, Joy, are among my closest friends, and he's even more fun off-screen than on-screen, if you can imagine that. I always look forward to spending time with them—they are both solid-gold people. We're on for dinner at Jean-Georges Restaurant, which is in the Trump International Hotel & Tower and is considered to be one of the finest restaurants in the world. With Jean-Georges Vongerichten in charge, how could it not be?

I take a call from Mark Burnett, the brilliant creator and producer of the reality show called *Survivor.* It was his idea to do *The Apprentice,* and we are busy working on the details.

11:30 A.M. I take a call from Sony; they'd asked me to be a sponsor for the 150th celebration of Central Park in July, featuring rising opera stars Salvatore Licitra and Marcello Alvarez. The event was a huge success, with many thousands of New Yorkers turning out to hear some magnificent singing on a perfect night under the stars in the park. On nights like that, you have to thank your own lucky stars just to be alive. We were all proud of how successful the evening was, and I was equally proud to be a sponsor.

Mike Donovan, my trusted pilot, calls in to update me on the checkup of my 727 jet. I have both a helicopter and a jet, and they get a workout throughout the year. With my schedule, they aren't luxury items, but necessities. Turns out the jet will be ready in two weeks.

Norma comes in to go over the media requests of the morning thus far, which include two from Holland, three from Germany, two from Canada, one from France, one from England, and seven from the United States. Handling media requests alone can require negotiation skills, and we do our best to accommodate them.

11:45 A.M. I have a meeting with Charlie Reiss, Jill Cremer, Russell Flicker, and Don Jr.—my development team. We are busy with a building in Chicago, and Don Jr. has been working very effectively and in many capacities on Trump Park Avenue. We have a lot on our plates already at The Trump Organization, but, not being a complacent type, I know there are many opportunities out there and this team tends to that. They do a great job and have some interesting projects to brief me about.

12:30 P.M. I order lunch from our terrific new restaurant at the Trump Tower atrium, which is doing great business. Some of you may have seen the commercial I did for McDonald's. I didn't have to act— I like McDonald's and am a loyal customer. Some days I have pizza, sometimes a ham and cheese, some days nothing, but I rarely go out for lunch. I still consider it an interruption in my workday. I review news clippings and articles during my lunch minute.

12:35 P.M. I speak to Bernd Lembcke, the director of the Mar-a-Lago Club. As you might remember, Mar-a-Lago was once my private home, and I restored it and turned it into a breathtaking private club. Anything that beautiful should be shared, and it has been an immense success. Bernd has tended to it, and I've been named to the Benefactors Board of Directors by the Historical Society of Palm Beach County. It's nice to see painstaking work being noticed and rewarded. We discuss the upcoming season and the latest improvements to the grounds.

12:45 P.M. I walk down the hall to visit George Ross. George will always tell you the way it is, which I appreciate. His thoughts are sharp and insightful, and we have a longish conversation of, perhaps, three minutes. I am thinking about putting him on *The Apprentice.*

12:50 P.M. Back in my office, I take a call from Hugh Grant. I had a brief role, as myself, in his movie with Sandra Bullock, *Two Weeks Notice.* Hugh's an avid golfer, and my course in Westchester is at his disposal whenever he's in New York. He's a nice guy on top of being a

With Allen Weisselberg, my CFO.

gifted actor. In fact, I'm glad he lives in another country—he's got too much on the ball to have around all the time.

1:00 P.M.   Norma comes in to go over the invitations to parties and openings, and for speeches. I don't have much time available. I decide on a party at Le Cirque.

1:30 P.M.   I put in a call to Trump National Golf Club in Los Angeles. This course is on the Pacific Ocean and has the potential to be better than Pebble Beach. "Spectacular" will be an understatement. It's a gem, and we're working hard on it. All is going well, but every detail is important and there are a lot of them to take care of.

2:30 P.M.   I make a call to an expert on trees. I saw some beautiful ones and would like to have them on my golf course in Bedminster, New Jersey. I ask a few questions and find out a lot. When I want to know something, I go for it, and only on rare occasions will I take a second-hand opinion. This tactic has served me well over the years—there's nothing wrong with knowledge, whether it's about trees or sinks.

3:00 P.M.   Allen Weisselberg, my CFO, comes in for a meeting. He's been with me for thirty years and keeps a handle on everything, which is not an easy job. He runs things beautifully. His team is tight and fast, and so are our meetings.

3:30 P.M.   I return the fourteen calls that came in during the meeting, which include those from lawyers, publishers, reporters, and friends. The only thing worse than having so many calls is not having any calls, so I'm not complaining.

I take a call from the concrete contractors, who have completely screwed up and are trying to tell me they haven't screwed up. Everything they've done is a mess. So instead of having the nice conversation they expected, I tell it to them the way it is—that they've made a mess of everything and they'd better get it right. The amazing thing is that they act like they know what they're doing. When people hear me yelling, believe me, there's a reason why.

4:30 P.M.   I go to the conference room for a photo session with Platon, a young and very accomplished photographer. The photos are for *Forbes* magazine. He is fast and efficient, very much like Richard Avedon was when I did a shoot with him last year. I look forward to seeing the prints.

5:00 P.M.   I return the seven calls received during the shoot, including one to my sister, Maryanne. She's still a judge and as wise as ever, and she has just returned from a trip to Rome.

5:30 P.M.   Norma comes in to go over more invitations and media requests, and I read a few letters. There's one from a nine-year-old boy in Minnesota who has a business proposal for me. After describing his business idea, he makes me a very tempting offer: "And what's in it for you, Mr. Trump? A chance for you to make millions, just by becoming my partner!" He also adds that I can call him anytime, as long as it's before 9:00 P.M. I'll keep that in mind.

6:00 P.M.   I decide to return to my apartment upstairs, where I make more calls, until 7:30 or so. At 8:00 P.M., Melania and I meet Joy and Regis at Jean-Georges Restaurant for a perfect meal.

TUESDAY

8:30 A.M.   I arrive at the office. I read between five and seven newspapers every morning before I get into the office. One thing I enjoy

At the Mar-a-Lago Club with Joy and Regis Philbin.

doing is clipping articles of interest, whether they're about me or not; then I either save or distribute them. I also receive between ten and twelve magazines a day, which I review in my apartment at the end of the day. Keeping up on things worldwide is of great importance if one is to keep the big picture in mind. Yes, I'm a New Yorker, but there's a big world out there and I try to stay informed about it. If you see the entire planet as an emerging market—which it is—you'll discover that you've got a lot of homework to do every day. It's not an indulgence, but an absolute necessity. So I spend the next fifteen minutes of relative quiet assessing world developments. Call it multitasking, call it whatever you will, it works and it focuses me for the day ahead.

8:45 A.M. I take a call from the guy trying to jack up the prices on the fixtures for a new building. Doesn't he know I *know* the market prices for everything I'm doing? These jerks think I don't do my homework—that's what it boils down to. Which means they're all in for a big surprise, and if I have to yell to get my point across, that's what I do.

9:00 A.M. I ask Rhona to call Bob Wright, the chairman and CEO of NBC. In addition to being a great admirer of his business acumen, I am friends with Bob and his wonderful wife, Suzanne. We've done some deals together, and in the seventeen years since he went from General Electric to NBC, the network has seen enormous improvements in quality control as well as growth in the right directions. Bob takes my call and we chat about a lot of things. Have you ever noticed that some people have a knack for enlightened conversation? Bob is one of those people. He's never been boring for one second of his life. I'm glad he takes the time to talk to me, and, considering his schedule, it's a good sign that maybe I don't bore him either.

Norma comes in to remind me that I have a Police Athletic League Board of Directors meeting next week. I am active with the Police Athletic League and have been for many years. They do a great job in New York and benefit many people and neighborhoods.

9:15 A.M. I take a call from Alfons Schmidt, who is someone I hold in very high esteem, not just because he's a great golfer and businessman, but because he's a remarkable person. Those who know him will agree with me. We'll meet on Friday for a round of golf at Trump National Golf Club in Briarcliff Manor. It's a high for me to play on the course with someone like Alfons. We'll be joined by former president Bill Clinton as well, who is a member. He lives nearby and likes the course, and we welcome him at any time. He's managed to become a good golfer, and, considering the schedule he had for so many years, that's saying something. If he keeps up this rate of improvement, he'll get really good very fast. Joining us will also be David Granger, the editor in chief of *Esquire,* a dapper guy on and off the golf course. It's a rare occasion that I take an afternoon off, but considering the company I'll be in, it will be worth it.

9:45 A.M. Ivanka, my beautiful daughter, calls to tell me about her most recent trip. She's on holiday and is taking off for somewhere else tomorrow. Keeping track of her isn't easy, but she's good about keeping me informed, and I'm happy she's enjoying herself. I'm a lucky guy with a daughter like this.

10:00 A.M. I have a board meeting in the conference room with Mark Brown and Bob Pickus from my Atlantic City team. John Burke and Scott Butera join us. We have these meetings every three months, to iron out any problems, to go over numbers, and to keep an eye on the future. Considering how large our operations are in Atlantic City— I have three casino hotels—our meetings are relatively brief; they rarely

*With Bill Clinton at Trump National Golf Club
in Briarcliff Manor, New York.*

last more than two hours. My team knows the value of time and exactly how not to waste it. People often comment on the brevity of my meetings, but if everyone knows what they're doing, they don't need to be long or long-winded. Fortunately, I have experienced people on my teams, and they know how I operate, so they get to the point, and quickly.

12:00 P.M. We have sandwiches from the Carnegie Deli in the boardroom. Ever had one of their ham-and-cheese or corned beef sandwiches? They're great. When you visit New York, try one.

12:15 P.M. I'm not antisocial, but to me, fifteen minutes is a very long lunch. So I'm back in my office, getting back to business, perusing the thirty-seven phone calls that came in during the meeting. These are the phone calls that have already been screened, first by the receptionist, and then by my assistants. I get hundreds of calls a day from around the world from people who just want to say hi or to tell me something. My security team takes some of the calls as well, because the number of calls can be overwhelming. But these are thirty-seven legitimate calls that must be dealt with, and I begin returning them. First I return Bob Kraft's call. He'd invited me to a private Elton John concert, which was terrific. Elton John just gets better and better; he's amazing. Bob Kraft is a first-class act all the way and always a delight to talk to. It's a good way to start the afternoon.

12:30 P.M. Joe Torre stops by for a surprise visit. He's the manager of the New York Yankees and always a welcome guest. He takes the time to sign autographs on his way in and on his way out. A real champ.

12:45 P.M. I return Rudy Giuliani's call. He was a great mayor, and he saw New York City through some difficult times. In addition to my respect for him professionally, we are also friends and we keep in touch. I will always wish him the best—and his wife, Judy, is tops!

1:00 P.M. The TV team from the National Geographic Channel are here for an interview. They've done great work, and I decide we should go up to my apartment for the interview. I don't often do that, but they are pros, and it goes very well. For the most part, I get along very well with media people. I respect them and the jobs they do, and they usually respect me and my time limits. It works both ways, and it's a rare occasion when we clash.

1:45 P.M. I take a call from Mohamed Al Fayed, the owner of Harrods in Knightsbridge, London, and the Ritz in Paris. He's one of a kind, a gentleman all the way, and I always make a point of visiting him when I'm in London. He's remained a kind and loyal person despite the tragedies in his life, and I am honored when he calls.

2:00 P.M. I call my brother, Robert. He's a great guy, and a good brother to have. We keep in close contact, and I consider myself lucky to have the brother and sisters that I've got.

Melania calls to remind me that we are going to see *Chicago* on Broadway tonight. I've seen it before, but Melanie Griffith is currently starring in it, and we want to see her. I already know she'll be terrific—she's a natural.

I return twelve calls in rapid succession, most of them concerning my different properties in New York and Florida. Each time, I ask what the problem is, and we get to it immediately. I like to keep a handle on all my properties, and the problems are to be expected. The time I worry the most is when there aren't any problems. That's usually the result of misinformation or wishful thinking on someone's part.

Here's one of my greatest wishes: I would like a computer chip that I could attach to the brains of all my contractors so they'd know exactly what I wanted, when I wanted it, and at what price. This would save me a lot of time, a lot of phoning, and a lot of yelling.

3:00 P.M.   I take a walk over to Trump Park Avenue, my new super-luxury building on Park Avenue and Fifty-ninth Street. This was the former Delmonico Hotel, which has historical merit, and the location is about as prime as you can get in New York. It's a prize building, and I make almost daily visits to see how it's progressing. I visit Laura Cordovano in the sales office, then check out the construction. They are taking too long, and the lobby doesn't look up to my standards yet. They get an earful, and they deserve it. When my name is on something, it'd better be great. Could it be any simpler?

It's funny, the reaction I get from people when I walk down the street and get recognized. Sometimes it's a double take, sometimes there's no acknowledgment, but often it's a wave and a familiar and friendly "Hi, Donald!" from total strangers. It still takes me by surprise. Once I was stuck in a horrible traffic jam in my limousine, and I had a few members of Mark Burnett's team with me, so I decided to try an experiment. It was one of those traffic jams where we hadn't moved an inch in ten minutes, and tempers were red-hot, with taxi drivers yelling and everyone else as well, and every car seemed to have its horn on permanent full blast. I decided to step out of my limousine and just stand there in the middle of this chaos. The reaction? At first, dead silence. Then the fuming drivers and passengers started waving and shouting "Donald! It's The Donald! Hi, Donald!" I had to laugh. At least we had some relief from the honking horns for a few minutes.

4:00 P.M.   Back in my office. I make a call downstairs, as I'd noticed some of the lobby door handles weren't as polished as I'd like them to be. I want my buildings to be impeccable, and the people who inhabit them appreciate that, even if I might seem a bit extreme at times.

I receive a letter from a U.S. serviceman overseas, Terry Simmons. His morale-building idea for his unit is to receive an autographed photograph from me. I am very touched by this request, and we send it off right away. These men and women are putting their lives on the line to protect something I cherish, which is this country. One of the great moments of my life was being honored, along with General John M. Keane, by the USO in 2002. In my speech I mentioned that accepting this honor put me in the finest company imaginable, because every member of the United States armed forces was being honored alongside me. I meant it then, and I still mean it today. We send our best to Terry Simmons.

4:30 P.M.   Giuseppe Cipriani, who has one of the best restaurants in New York, calls. As someone who goes out to dinner a lot, I have very particular tastes, and Giuseppe is someone who will never let you down. I am trying to get him into my Park Avenue building.

The mysterious Jeffrey calls in. As mysterious as Jeffrey is, he's one of the few people I know who can get by on just a first name. My staff never asks for a last name in his case, which in a way puts him up there with Elvis. Not that Elvis calls in much these days, but you never know. That's why I have a floor for security. Sometimes we need it. We've had some calls you wouldn't believe.

Norma comes in to tell me she's had it with *The Apprentice* TV crew looking like "ragamuffins" and that if they show up tomorrow in their usual gear she's going to send them back to their hotel "to dress properly for a change." She means business and I know it, so I try to explain that they're from California and working on a TV-show set, not in our corporate office, but she'll have none of it. I think they're in for it, and I don't envy them.

I call Vinnie Stellio, a longtime employee whose wife has just had a baby boy. Vinnie could've been a movie star with his looks and swagger, but, fortunately, he works for us. He also could've written his own scripts, but he's busy enough as it is.

5:00 P.M. I call Arnold Schwarzenegger to congratulate him on his recent decision to run for governor of California. I've also received several media calls asking me for my opinion on his decision. I've always liked Arnold, and I think he'll make a great governor, not just because I like him but because he's got the smarts and energy to run a state like California.

I read an article by a journalist who spent a day with me a few months ago. I remember him saying that he felt one day wouldn't be sufficient, and I remember telling him that most people felt that one day with me was enough. At the end of the article, he admits I was right—that one day with me was enough—he was completely exhausted. It's funny, because to me it seemed like a more relaxing and low-key day than I usually have, and I was certainly on my best behavior. Anyway, it's nice to be right.

5:30 P.M. Norma comes in to review media requests, charity requests, and invitations. Since September 11, requests for charity have increased sharply, and we do what we can. We comment on how we receive a consistently high number of letters from Canada. One letter is from two ladies in Saskatchewan who have invited me to have a cup of coffee with them at their local coffeehouse, which has two tables. If I decide to accept, they will do their best to reserve a table for me. Due to my schedule, I have to decline, but their offer is genuine and kind, and if I had the time, I'd go.

Sometimes I answer media requests myself, when I have time. Once I called a guy named Phil Grande in Florida. He has a small radio program, *Stock Trading & Money Talk*, and he had faxed me an interview request. I picked up the phone and called him myself. When he asked who was calling, I said, "Donald Trump," and he said, "Yeah, and I'm J. P. Morgan." It took some convincing on my part, but he finally believed me, and we chatted for some time. Afterward, he called my assistants to verify that I had indeed called him, and to this day he sends them flowers every Christmas. People like Phil can make our jobs a lot of fun.

6:00 P.M. Asprey, the jewelers who occupy the corner of Trump Tower on Fifth Avenue, are expanding, and they've invited me down to see the renovations. They will have three floors, and it will be stunning—much like their jewelry. They are the jewelers to the royal family in England, and their new space will reflect that status when it's done. I also decide to check on my new tenants, Mark Burnett Productions, on the way down to the lobby, to see that everything is up to par. I have a great management team, but I like to check things out for myself as much as possible. I make a quick call to Melania to check on dinner plans before the theater, and I leave the office.

WEDNESDAY

9:00 A.M. Melanie Griffith was terrific in *Chicago* last night, and we visited her afterward to tell her so.

I take a call regarding placing antennas on The Trump Building at 40 Wall Street. Since the World Trade Towers are gone, 40 Wall Street is once again the tallest building in lower Manhattan. It's not a fact that particularly appeals to me, but it is a fact. Whatever will best serve the Financial District is fine with me.

Melania Knauss

I have to say one thing about New Yorkers, and that is that after September 11, they just continued to move forward and do their best. That took courage, and I think it shows what makes New York City such a great place.

I place a call to Governor Pataki, and take a call from John Myers, president of GE Asset Management. We've done some deals together and he's a great guy—and a very smart one.

9:30 A.M. Kevin Harris, a supervising producer for Mark Burnett, is ready to take me on a tour of the sets built in Trump Tower for *The Apprentice*. He has on some sort of a new vintage bowling shirt, deconstructed jeans with more holes than fabric, and some very original footwear that I can't begin to describe. This guy could make Helmut Lang look old hat, but we make a quick getaway before Norma can see him.

The construction site also includes living quarters for the sixteen contestants, which is an incredibly stylish ten-thousand-square-foot loft, probably the only such living space in midtown. I am pleasantly surprised at the quality of the work, and my trust in Mark Burnett is again confirmed.

10:00 A.M. Back in my office, I begin returning calls. People are surprised at how many hours I put in at my office each week, since I seem to have a busy social life as well. I also like to plan my business trips for the weekends whenever possible, to avoid missing office time. I love what I do, so it doesn't seem like I'm missing out on any fun. Last year I took a transatlantic weekend business trip that included breakfast in London with Mohamed Al Fayed and dinner in Slovenia with Melania's parents before flying back to New York. We were back in time for me to be in the office by 9:00 A.M. Monday.

I talk to Jay Goldberg, a brilliant lawyer and an old friend. He and his wife, Rema, will join me in my box at the U.S. Open.

This is a good one: The pushiest broker in New York calls in for a chat about the availability of some of my prime apartments, as if I couldn't guess why she was calling me in the first place. She tries to tell me what my apartments are worth, and I try to control my temper, but she's full of bullshit. Finally, I ask her if she realizes who she's talking to and, surprisingly, she immediately becomes reasonable. Almost every day, I have to remind someone that maybe I know what I'm doing, and while that may sound like I'm tooting my own horn, believe me, it saves a lot of yelling time.

10:30 A.M. The German TV team is ready for an interview in the conference room. They'd done a wonderful job in covering Mar-a-Lago a few months ago, which I appreciate, and so we're doing a New York interview. They are professional and enthusiastic, and all goes well. You see, I've done so many interviews that at times they can be boring for me, so if the people are interesting, it helps a lot. Just this year, both of my sons did their first TV interviews, and that was exciting. The *Today* show did a Father's Day program, and Matt Lauer interviewed Don Jr. and myself, which was great fun. Both Matt Lauer and Katie Couric have a knack for making anything entertaining, and I enjoy them tremendously. *48 Hours* interviewed my younger son, Eric, and myself, and aside from some slumping on his part, Eric did a great job. The media really isn't anything new to my kids, although they've been protected from it to a certain extent.

11:00 A.M. I receive an invitation to attend the show of Oscar de la Renta's new collection, and I call Melania. We decide to attend. I've never gotten tired of fashion or fashion shows. To me, it's an unbeatable combination—beautiful women and beautiful clothes, especially Oscar's.

My agency, Trump Model Management, has managed to put itself on the fashion map in a relatively short time. I started it about five years ago. We've got some top models, and I enjoy watching this business become more and more successful. I call John Tutolo for an update, and we discuss a few things that we think could be improved.

I call Paula Shugart, president of the Miss Universe Organization, to go over a few things with her. An interviewer recently asked me what motivated me to buy the rights to the Miss Universe pageant. My answer was that I love beautiful women and I'm also a businessman, so it seemed like a good idea, which it has turned out to be. Sometimes things are that simple. I realized early on that I was an aesthete by nature, being attracted to beauty in both people and buildings. My work has shown that some early self-knowledge was right on target.

I take a call from Ricardo Bellino, a businessman in Brazil. We are working on the Villa Trump together in Brazil, and he's also asking me some questions for his upcoming book on the power of ideas. I mention that ideas are door openers, the first step. Without a first step, there won't be any other steps to take you where you want to go. It's a visual process. Perhaps that's why I'm a visionary, but a well-grounded one. When it comes to great ideas, the first questions I ask myself are: *Yeah, but is it possible? Will this be feasible?* If I can see something being accomplished, I know it is a possibility. I guess that's why I'm a builder. I start from the ground and go up from there.

I write a congratulatory note to Kitty Carlisle Hart for her ninety-third birthday. In addition to being multitalented, she's been a true philanthropist, and New York is lucky to have her. I always liked to watch her on television. Those of you who remember the television show *To Tell the Truth* will know what I'm talking about.

I write another note to a high school that has asked me for advice, and also asked who my favorite U.S. president might be. I decide to start with a quote by Abraham Lincoln, who would have to be my first choice: "I will study and prepare, and perhaps my chance will come." Always humble, always hardworking, always studying, Lincoln is a great example for high school kids.

11:30 A.M. The Entertainment Channel is ready for an interview regarding *The Apprentice*. It goes quickly and well, and we're done in five minutes.

12:00 P.M. I call an employee at a large property who has not been as attentive as his position demands. I tell him that his bad performance is not his fault, but mine: I simply hired the wrong person by overestimating his capabilities. I add that if he'd like to change my mind about my initial mistake, it's up to him. He promises to take care of things right away, and I think he means it.

I ask Andy Weiss to come in. His office is about 110 feet down the hall, but he can hear me. The reason we don't have an intercom system is because we don't need one. This often startles visitors, but, as I see it, why have more gadgets than necessary? Andy's been with me a long time, and we get right to the point. The meeting's over in less than five minutes.

I call Beverly Sills, one of the most wonderful opera singers of all time, and an equally wonderful person. I may not enjoy sitting through an opera, but I have always respected opera singers and enjoy the highlights of opera. Beverly is remarkable in every way, and I always enjoy talking to her.

12:30 P.M. I decide to have a slice of pizza for lunch, and I read a few of the letters that have come in. Here's one from a young man in the

Bay Area of San Francisco who writes, "This letter is in appreciation for inspiring us in hard times. Please continue writing your books and influencing people to live their dreams." He'll be happy to know that's exactly what I'm doing, even as I eat my pizza and read his letter. Here's another one from a family in Germany, who thinks I should run for president and invites me to stay at their home. A business proposal comes from a group in Wales who would like me to work on a housing development with them.

12:45 P.M.   I call Brian Baudreau, my executive of security, and tell him I want to go over to Trump Place, my development along the Hudson River. We go over to the West Side and check out what's going on with construction. We meet with Paul Davis, the CEO of the Hudson Waterfront Associates, and take a walk around. I get daily reports, but there's nothing like seeing things for yourself. Paul has a big project on his hands, and he's doing a terrific job.

I've encountered a lot of opposition from staunch West Siders about this development, but gradually they are beginning to see that these buildings will be an enhancement to their neighborhood. The West Side is thriving like never before, and even as an East Sider, I've got to admit that the West Side is a great place to be.

2:00 P.M.   Back in the office, I start returning the twenty-two calls that came in. That's another reason I don't like to be out of the office too much—the backlog of calls can get out of hand. The first call I return is to United Cerebral Palsy, as I'm on the advisory board. One of the biggest perks of being financially successful is being able to be generous. I like giving money to good causes like United Way and the Police Athletic League. It really is a great feeling every time I can be of help, and, for the most part, that's a private part of my life. Some of my charities are public knowledge, and some of them aren't.

2:30 P.M. Robin Leach and his team are here for an interview. Robin is well known for a reason. We have a great time, and it's a job well and quickly done.

3:15 P.M. I have a meeting with Carolyn Kepcher, executive vice president and director of Trump National Golf Club in Briarcliff. We are building some magnificent villas on the grounds, and there are a lot of details to attend to. Fortunately, both of us are perfectionists, and our meetings never have to be long.

3:30 P.M. I take a call from David Schner, president of *Leaders* magazine. I'd been interviewed a few months back and we still keep in touch.

Craig Semandl, the director of Trump National Golf Club, Los Angeles, calls in. He gives me an update on what's happening, and we go over some details. I will visit California later this month to see the progress for myself. It helps to have people you can trust when you're three thousand miles away.

This is something that still amazes me: Here's another person requesting my autograph on the March 1990 issue of *Playboy* magazine, which featured an interview and a cover photo of me. To this day, thirteen years later, I receive several requests a month for my autograph on this issue, and, granted, the girl I'm photographed with is a beauty, but I never thought this interview would remain so popular with people who follow my career. I'll have to reread it one of these days. Meanwhile, I sign the cover and it's sent back to the owner, and I sign a few books that have been sent in as well.

I make a call to Tiffany, my youngest daughter, who is giving me an update on her latest activities. She has enough going on for five people. She must take after me. She is excited about her upcoming birthday and her plans to have a party aboard the *Queen Mary* in Long Beach, California.

I write a note to the Veterans of Vietnam of Ward 4CD of Valley Forge General Hospital. I am cochairman and builder of the New York Vietnam Veterans Memorial Fund, and still continue to do what I can for these brave people.

4:00 P.M. I take a call from Susan James, director of sales for Trump International Hotel and Tower on Central Park West. She has a great job—this is one of the most successful condominium towers ever built and the top-rated luxury hotel in New York City, all in one building. This is also where Jean-Georges Restaurant is located. All in all, it's a gem, and I'm proud of it. It's near Lincoln Center on Columbus Circle, and those of you who know architecture will find it interesting that Philip Johnson designed both this building and the State Theatre at Lincoln Center, home of the New York City Ballet. I'm sort of young to be considered historical, but some things point in that direction, and this building is one of those things.

I go over the invitations and requests of the day with Norma. I decide on an event given by Anna Wintour of *Vogue* magazine and leave the other decisions until later, when I can give them more time and consideration.

Charlie Reiss comes in and we go over current project developments in Chicago, Toronto, and London. Bernie Diamond and Jason Greenblatt, my terrific in-house attorneys, are in on the meeting as well. Contrary to what people may think, I listen to and take advice from a lot of people before I make a final decision on anything. I like to be as well informed as possible. However, when it comes to making a decision, I am aware that the full responsibility for that decision is, and will always remain, mine. That is why I proceed with caution, even if my image may be more flamboyant.

4:30 P.M. I have a meeting with Matthew Calamari, my chief of operations. He's always a busy guy, but with *The Apprentice* starting up soon, he's busier than ever. I'm not concerned, because after knowing Matthew for more than twenty years, I am certain he can handle anything.

My son Eric stops by to say hello. He's in college now but is visiting New York City for a couple of days. He sits in on my meeting with Matthew and then we chat for a bit. He's got a great grin. I love it when my kids visit, and we decide to have dinner together tonight.

5:15 P.M. I write a welcome-back letter to the members of the Mar-a-Lago Club. We are finishing a new ballroom, and it will be magnificent. One visitor to the Mar-a-Lago Club remarked that F. Scott Fitzgerald and his friends would feel right at home there. I had to agree. I'm looking forward to the new season, and I fly down most weekends during the winter.

I return a few calls, including one to Larry King, one of the sharpest interviewers of all time; another to a reporter for the *Star-Ledger* in New Jersey; and one to a reporter doing a story on the wonderful and very smart Russell Simmons.

John Myers, the president and CEO of GE Asset Management, calls in. He's a terrific guy in every sense of the word, and we are active together with the Damon Runyon Cancer Foundation, along with Dale Frey, who preceded John at GE and likewise did an absolutely fantastic job. These are two guys worth knowing. Over the years, General Electric has been my partner in a number of my developments, including the very successful Trump International Hotel and Tower at 1 Central Park West.

6:00 P.M.   I call Melania to see where we should take Eric for dinner. We decide on the "21" Club.

Norma comes in and we review some details of my deals, invitations, letters, and media requests, including those from a surprising number of international television programs and publications. Last year I did an interview for the number one program in China, which drew a huge audience. These facts continue to surprise me, probably because I am so focused on my immediate and daily responsibilities. I never found myself to be particularly fascinating.

The phones have quieted down, so I decide to go through a box I keep beside my desk where I put articles and letters of interest to me. Sometimes I'll keep certain articles for years if I like them. I also keep letters and quotes, such as "Hope is not a strategy." I saved an invitation from a speech I gave to the Wharton Business School Club about the future of New York City. I am always honored to speak to Wharton students and alumni.

I find nice notes from Dr. Jerry Buss of the Los Angeles Lakers, one terrific guy; Ed Malloy, an old friend I call "Blue Eyes"; and Harrison Tucker LeFrak, the next generation in a remarkable real estate family. Richard LeFrak, the son of Sam LeFrak, has done an amazing job in the real estate business. Likewise, his son Harrison will be one of the really great young people to watch. I have no doubt he will go right to the top.

There's a clipping from Liza Minnelli and David Gest's wedding, which I was honored to attend, even though I didn't think the mar-

"To Donald Trump—'I wanna be like you when I grow up.' Shaq."

riage had a chance, and letters from John F. Kennedy Jr. and Howard Schultz of Starbucks, as well as one from Clint Eastwood, a great guy and golfer. He was my guest at Mar-a-Lago. He liked my course in Florida and wrote to tell me that.

I come across a fax from Roger Ailes of Fox Network News. What a job he's done, taking them to heights they'd probably never dreamed of.

During the march toward war in Iraq, someone sent me this joke: "You know the world has changed when you realize the best rapper is a white guy, the best golfer is a black guy, and Germany doesn't want to go to war."

A review to savor, from Rick Remsnyder upon the opening of Trump National Golf Course: "Trump National's par 3 thirteenth hole, which features a breathtaking 100-foot man-made waterfall behind the green, is one of the most challenging and spectacular holes in the world." Music to my ears.

I love sports. I have one of Shaquille O'Neal's oversized sneakers on display in my office and a signed baseball from my favorite team, the New York Yankees. I keep it near Tiffany's drawing of a house. She's already into real estate.

Speaking of real estate: I've saved an article about how I sold the land under the Empire State Building for $57.5 million in March 2002. New York real estate can be a wonderful business. I've also clipped a profile of another great success story, developer Steve Witkoff, who owns the Woolworth Building and the News Building, in addition to valuable property in London. In an interview with a London newspaper, Steve described me as "the only real estate person in this world who can brand his name individually. In my opinion, it's not going to happen again. Donald is a master at marketing. But you can't market and be a master at marketing unless you've got great product—it doesn't work like that. They say 'Coke are masters at marketing Coke,' or 'Nike, they're masters at marketing Nike.' You know what? They've got the best drink and the best sneakers. Well, Donald develops the best buildings. It's a fact of life. He's a great developer. No one wants to give him credit for that."

Finally, I come across a postcard from my gorgeous daughter Ivanka and an old postcard from my parents. I miss them. I still have two-thirds of the box to go through, but I'm on for dinner with Eric and Melania and I don't want to be late.

7:00 P.M.   I pick up a large pile of documents to take with me, say good night to Norma, turn off the lights, leave my office, and head up to my apartment. It's been a good day. Business tip: Keep a box by your desk for mementos of the people and events that matter in your life and career. Reviewing the contents every now and then will keep you aware of your good fortune.

THURSDAY

8:30 A.M.   This morning I have an interview with the legendary Barbara Walters, regarding the upcoming anniversary of September 11. All goes well; she's professional and to the point, which always helps. I am also planning a surprise visit this morning to Barbara's show, *The View*, as I have been the center of their discussions for a few days. They've been waiting for me to call them, which I haven't done, as I think a personal appearance might be more fun, although they don't know about it yet. If someone challenges you, always try to take the challenge and run with it.

9:15 A.M. I have a meeting with Elaine Diratz, the director of sales at Trump World Tower at the United Nations Plaza. This condominium tower experienced a lot of opposition while it was being built, but it has literally been a triumph, both nationally and internationally. Even though Herbert Muschamp of *The New York Times* has lauded it and it has recently won a coveted European award for design, that doesn't mean we sit back in wonder at our good fortune. Everything requires upkeep, especially something of this caliber—plus it is in constant demand as a location site for films and television shows. Elaine and I troubleshoot the latest details.

9:45 A.M. Don Jr. comes in to update me on his work. He's sharp and has some good insights on a few of our developments. It makes me think that maybe he's paid attention all these years after all. Norma comes in to tell me I should get going.

10:00 A.M. Brian and I go over to the ABC studios on the West Side, to tape a special segment with Regis Philbin. It's a beautiful day and the city is sparkling—and as ever, so are Regis and Kelly.

11:00 A.M. I am lurking in the studios of Barbara Walters's show *The View*, where I see Sharon Stone, who is a scheduled guest. At the top of the program, they are still discussing my hair and why I haven't called them back. Joy Behar mentions that here she is, still waiting for some guy to call, and Meredith Vieira mentions that expecting Donald Trump to call her back might be expecting too much. This conversation continues for a while—will he call?, won't he call?—and then I decide to just walk out onto the set. The audience shrieks when they see me, and Joy is, well, not exactly overjoyed but certainly surprised. I receive a very warm welcome from Barbara, Star, and Meredith, and I think Joy is relieved to know that I'm not at all in a huff over her remarks. I even let her touch and rearrange my hair and explain that while it may not be great hair, it's mine, and it's fine with me. We have a good time, and I think we'll all have to agree that a visit is better than a phone call.

12:00 P.M.   Steve Wynn is here to visit me. We chat for a while and then I take him on a tour of *The Apprentice* sets being built downstairs. Steve and I are close friends—again!

12:30 P.M.   This is an unusual day, even for me. Sandra Bullock is here to visit, so she comes into the conference room where I'm having a meeting, just to say hi. I think the guys in the room are very impressed, and so am I, but I try to act cool. After all, my life isn't exactly dull, but getting a visit from Sandra is a highlight for everyone—especially the contractors, who cannot believe that it is actually her.

1:00 P.M.   Robin, one of my assistants, is eating a great-looking salad, so I ask her to order one for me. Then I start returning calls that came in while I was out, including one to Bob Tisch, owner of the Giants and Loews Hotels. The Tisch family has been a tremendous force for good in New York City, and I like Bob a lot. Most of the people I know don't take lunch hours, so when I return calls at lunchtime it means I actually want to talk to them.

I talk to Ashley Cooper, director of Trump National Golf Club at Bedminster, New Jersey, for an update on progress. I'll visit next week by helicopter to check things out for myself.

I call Sirio Maccioni, the owner of Le Cirque, one of my favorite restaurants in New York. We've decided to have a business dinner there tonight; while getting a table isn't a problem, I like to talk to Sirio just to catch up on things. He has the instincts required to run a great restaurant, as well as the manners. I always look forward to seeing him.

1:30 P.M.   I see Norma in the small conference room, meeting with the Bank One executives about a credit card, the Trump card, which I am starting. Everyone tells me this will be a great success, and it is going very well.

Aretha Franklin's assistant calls to see if I can attend her concert at Radio City later in the month. Aretha is one of the all-time greats, but, unfortunately, I will be out of town on business. That's one of the downsides of having a busy schedule, but it's flattering to hear from Aretha.

One of the things I think about when my schedule gets a little crazy is a labyrinth. Labyrinths date back to the ancient Greeks and usually imply something intricate or complex. Thinking about them helps me, because my schedule can make a labyrinth look like tic-tac-toe, so it becomes a soothing visual for me. That may be some convoluted psychology, but it works. Later on, I learned that there are some famous labyrinths still around today, such as the one at Chartres Cathedral, in France, and that they serve some meditative purpose, but the motive for me has always been to gain perspective on my own agenda.

As they say, whatever works.

2:00 P.M.   I attend the board meeting for one of my residential properties in the small conference room. I think anyone who lives in any of my buildings is fortunate, not just to be in a great building, but because we take pride in upkeep and service. We try to cater to the people living and working in my buildings in every way possible, so these meetings are important to me, and here's the reason: Past, present, and future tenants and owners have one very important quality in common. They all want the best for their money, which allows me to give you a simple formula for success: Deliver the goods.

A lady in a building across from one of mine actually called in to complain to us. Her complaint? The constant cleaning and polishing of my building was making her crazy. Every time she looked outside and across the street, someone was cleaning something, which she thought was excessive and unnecessary, and that I must have some sort of a problem that should be taken care of. Ever hear of New York stories? The funny part is that we don't have to make them up.

2:45 P.M.   I decide to take a tour of the office. First I visit Bernie Diamond, my general counsel, who is conferring with Sonja Talesnik. Then I see Andy Weiss and Don Jr. about something they're working on. I pass Scott Etess, who is on the phone, and see Charlie, Jill, and Russell in the conference room. I stop by to visit Micha Koeppel, VP of construction, and notice that Nathan Nelson and Anna DeVincentis are both busy on their phones. I ask my accounting team, Jeff McConney and Eric Sacher, to meet with me and Allen Weisselberg at 4:30. I see Ramon dealing with an enormous pile of mail, which we get plenty of around here. Everyone looks busy to me, and there's a nice hum to all the activity. On my way back, I stop to chat with George Ross and Jason Greenblatt. I notice some doorknobs need polishing and that the copy room needs to be cleaned up a bit, but on the whole, the office is looking good. We've been in our Trump Tower offices for twenty years, and they still look brand-new.

3:00 P.M.   I agree to go to Ferragamo's new store opening and the Luca Luca fashion show at Bryant Park, and we're trying to arrange my weekend schedule, which at this point is a whirlwind, even with a helicopter. It's a good thing I'm an active type, or this might tire me out.

Reggie Jackson stops by for a quick visit. He is always welcome here, and my staff loves it when he visits. We chat for a few minutes, and I remember all the incredible moments he has given us as a Yankee. Truly a great.

I return calls to Jay Neveloff, David Scharf, and my brother Robert, and make a call to Wollman Rink to see how we did with our summer attraction, Victorian Gardens. We used the ice rink space as an upscale amusement park for children during the summer months, and since this is our first season doing so, I'm interested in a firsthand account.

3:30 P.M.   I take a walk over to Trump Park Avenue, at Park and Fifty-ninth. As I said, I like to keep my eye on things, and I never find property checks tedious. This is such a beautiful building. I remember being interviewed last year by *The New York Times* about both the building itself and the real estate market in New York. I told them "People would rather invest in real estate than in Enron and WorldCom. You can touch it, feel it, smell it. As opposed to Enron, which you can only smell." Costas Kondylis mentioned that this building also had an advantage over properties that boast of being prewar-like, in that this building is definitely not prewar-like. It *is* prewar. Anyway, the work is coming along and it's looking good.

I guess someone saw *The View* on TV this morning, because, as I'm walking back, a lady says "Hey, Donald! Your hair looks great!" Whoever you are, thanks.

4:30 P.M.   I take a call from Joe Cinque regarding Sardinia. That's pretty far away but he says that next to Mar-a-Lago, it's his favorite place, and this guy travels all over the world. I'll have to check into it a bit.

I have a short meeting with my finance group, Allen, Jeff, and Eric. I should have a picture of these guys for you—what a crew! However, they do good work. People often ask me where I find the people who work for me. I think it must be divine intervention, if there is such a thing. But somehow, it all works. Remember how I once said that you should try to get people you like to work for you? These guys are a good example of that advice.

4:50 P.M. Rhona comes in to tell me that Jim Griffin is on the line. Ever heard of the William Morris Agency? He's the guy to know. Jim is another example of someone who will always tell it like it is, which I appreciate. He'll give you the facts, and fast.

5:00 P.M. I get a lot of letters from students of all ages who ask me specific things—either for school projects or for their own interest—and, while I can't respond to them all, I like to review their letters. Sometimes the simplicity and directness of their questions can keep me aware of small and simple things. As Benjamin Franklin once said, "Beware of little expenses. A small leak will sink a great ship." In business, nothing is ever too small to notice.

5:30 P.M. I review a pile of legal documents, making short notes on them for response by my assistants tomorrow morning. If we didn't keep up with our correspondence several times a day, we'd be sunk. I receive requests from people in every industry under the sun, moon, and stars combined. My daily delivery includes submissions from artists, musicians, screenwriters, architects, authors, poets, comedians, chefs, designers, actors, shoemakers, and more. That's a condensed list. I also receive bundles of cookbooks from a lady in Illinois several times a year. Why she does this is beyond me. She must know that one of the few things I don't do is cook.

6:30 P.M. Enough ruminating. I check my faxes and go upstairs.

FRIDAY

8:30 A.M. The electrical contractors call in with some bogus claims about why they're way off schedule. They've been slacking off on the job. I've been watching them carefully and know exactly what their problem is, and proceed to tell them so. They get the message and promise me they will get back on track. We'll see. I believe about twenty percent of what contractors say, and that's on a good day. They know what I mean.

9:00 A.M. I take a call from Dick Levy, a real gentleman, then I ask for a Diet Coke. Another call concerns an ad I placed about slot machines at the racetracks in New York, which I'm against. Without countless layers of security, it will not be in the public's best interest, and I therefore mention that it is obvious the ground under our racetracks is most fertile for growing organized crime. The ad contains a photograph of Al Capone, with the caption "He would have loved it." The bottom of the ad says, "Paid for by a Committee of one, who may not always be right, but knows what's wrong." I think the point is made.

Rhona asks about the Giants game next week, and I decide to go. I return calls from Bo Dietl, Vinnie Stellio, and Ivana, and place a call to Jim Griffin of the William Morris Agency. David Granger calls; *Esquire* magazine is using an apartment in Trump World Tower as an example of the ultimate man's apartment, the Esquire Apartment. I have to agree with him that it's the ideal place.

I take a call from a writer doing an article on motivation and leadership. One of the questions asked is how I handle a person who consistently makes the same mistakes. I tell them the truth: I don't. They're working for someone else now.

9:30 A.M. I take a moment to glance out the window, which I rarely do, even with the spectacular views from my office. There is something inspiring about New York City, and I feel fortunate to live here. Just as I'm thinking this, a call comes in from *Los Angeles Confidential Magazine* for a comment on their publication. I tell them that Los Angeles is as viable a cosmopolitan center as New York City, which it is, and that I think their magazine has a lot of integrity. I always enjoy my trips to California, and with my new golf course in Los Angeles, I'll be able to spend more time there in the near future. I decide to call Jason Binn, just to catch up on things with him. He's a successful magazine publisher, and I haven't spoken to him for a couple of weeks. I enjoy his take on things.

Tom Fazio calls in to go over some course plans and to give me an update on my New Jersey golf course. He loves what he does and that's made apparent by his attention to detail. John Mack of Credit Suisse calls in. Despite his great accomplishments, he remains an unassuming man—the work is what matters to him. These are two easy and informative calls. People have to understand that I've been dealing with all kinds of people and industries for a long time, so I can pretty readily discern who the goof-offs are and who the solid-gold people are. So if you hear me blow up in my office at someone or something, there's usually a reason for it. It can be as clear as day to me, and I see no reason to tolerate someone being inefficient or irresponsible. I do my best, and so should they.

I heard someone who had worked with me for a long time describing me as a generator—someone who revs up, keeps going, gathers momentum, keeps going at a higher level, and all is well—except for the boiling point. Because when something causes me to explode, believe me, there will be a lot of energy behind it. But, hey, at least I can be honest about it, and his assessment is accurate. A great Palm Beach lawyer called me a reverse tornado—I build everything in my path, instead of destroying it.

Robin comes in to tell me the copies I want are delayed because our copy machine is on the blink again. I can't believe it. With all the amazing inventions of today, can't they design a copy machine that won't break down every three minutes? This is one thing that can make me lose my temper. I personally call Pete Strada, our director of purchasing, and ask him when the lease is up on this terrible machine. I want it out of here.

10:00 A.M. Norma comes in and we go over the event I'm hosting with Heidi Klum and Jonathan Tisch for the Elizabeth Glaser Pediatric AIDS Foundation. It will be held at Sotheby's next month. We also discuss some interview requests and invitations, seeing if and how we can fit them into my schedule. Every week we think that week can't be topped, then the next week is even more hectic, so what's happened is that our stamina has increased. I am much busier now than I have ever been. That's one reason I don't complain much. I literally don't have time to.

I take a call from Tony Senecal, the head butler and historian at Mar-a-Lago. This guy is terrific and a great asset to Mar-a-Lago. He fills me in on the latest, and I'm glad he has X-ray vision when it comes to details.

Jean-Georges Vongerichten calls in. In addition to being a genius when it comes to food, he's also a visionary. He's a celebrity in his own right, but I can tell you that what really matters to him is cooking—and when you visit any of his restaurants, you'll find out what I mean.

10:30 A.M. Tina Brown, of publishing fame, calls. We weren't always on such good terms, but we put our differences aside. I enjoy talking with her. She's quick and insightful.

I ask George Ross and Carolyn Kepcher to come in. I've decided they should play themselves in pivotal roles on *The Apprentice*. They both agree and do not seem put out at all. There won't be any acting involved, because to them it will be another day on the job. Maybe a longer day on the job, but just another day. Total pros.

I take a call from Jim Dowd, senior press manager at NBC, regarding *The Apprentice,* and one from Jay Bienstock, a producer on *The Apprentice.* Both guys know exactly what they're doing, which is a relief to me. Then I yell at some contractors for a while. It's too boring to tell you about this, but it's something that is absolutely necessary in real estate development and construction. I spend much of my days doing this.

I take a call from Eliot Spitzer, the New York State attorney general. He is one smart guy, who has an even more brilliant future ahead of him. He is just amazing!

11:00 A.M. I go down to the large conference room to see some plans for a possible new development. Charlie, Russell, Jill, and Don Jr., my development team, go over them with me. This could be a go, but I'll have to think about it a bit more. I don't have a formula for making decisions—each situation is unique, and I allow my assessment to be equally unique, with no time constraints. When it's right, it will be right. I may have the reputation of being brash, but I am very restrained in regard to making decisions. People don't see the process—they only see the results.

11:30 A.M. I return nine calls and realize I'm looking forward to having lunch at the golf club and a round of golf with Bill Clinton, David Granger, and Alfons. It's a beautiful day, and I love checking out the course. That's one reason I don't feel too guilty about taking a Friday afternoon off—I'll still be working.

Someone sends in a big box of Godiva chocolates. This will be tough, but I'll just look at them for a while and then put them outside for my staff. Who says I'm not a nice guy? Ditto for those Belgian truffles. Life can be tough.

12:00 P.M.   I ask George Ross to come in, and we go over a few things. George brings the word *laconic* to life. Five minutes with him equals one hour with your average lawyer.

12:05 P.M.   I decide to call Mike Donovan. I want to see how the work is going on my 727. He says it will be ready next week, which is good news, as I want to visit my golf course in California.

12:15 P.M.   Mark Burnett and his two producers, Jay Bienstock and Kevin Harris, come in for a meeting, to go over the assignments to be given to the sixteen candidates on *The Apprentice*. This is an interesting process. We want to make sure that each assignment has a purpose beyond entertainment. These guys are not only nice, they're intelligent. I really feel they've got their bases covered. Any apprehensions I had about the TV show have evaporated.

12:45 P.M.   I go through twenty-seven requests, including invitations from Norway, Peru, and India. Norma tells me I should view the video made for Trump Park Avenue before I leave, which has some beautiful footage. It's a great video.

1:00 P.M.   I collect my papers and faxes and ask Rhona to call the elevator and to tell Eddie to have the car ready in fifteen minutes.

I make my exit. It's been a great week. I just hope the car is ready. Otherwise, Eddie's in for it—big time.

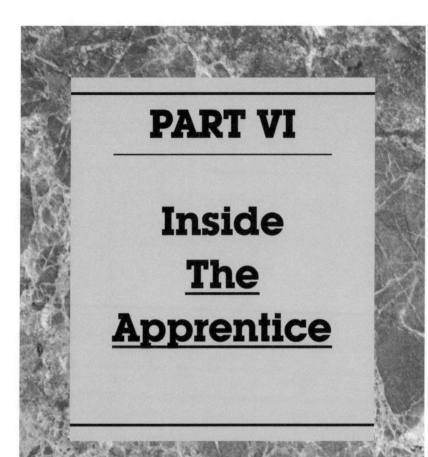

PART VI

Inside
The
Apprentice

Here I am with Mark Burnett, creator of The Apprentice, *and Jeff Zucker, president of NBC Entertainment.*

Prime Time

Over the past few years, since reality shows came into vogue, television networks have been trying to get me to do one. They approached me with offers for substantial amounts of money, but the concept was always predictable. They wanted to follow me around with cameras, watching me make deals, brush my teeth, and, most certainly, comb my hair. None of this appealed to me at all.

One day, I was approached by the head of CBS Entertainment, Les Moonves, who wanted to broadcast the live finale of the hit series *Survivor* from Wollman Rink in Central Park, which I control through a long-term lease. It sounded like a great idea to me, especially when they told me they were going to build a jungle to replicate the one in which the *Survivor* contestants had been living.

When I arrived at Wollman Rink that night, I was amazed to see what they had been able to do. They had transformed a city skating rink into an exotic wildlife scene. As I was heading toward my seat, an attractive young man approached me and said, "Hi, Mr. Trump, I'm Mark Burnett and I'm the creator of *Survivor.*"

I said, "Mark, you don't have to tell me that. Everybody knows who you are, but it's really nice to meet you."

He said, "You know, Mr. Trump, I have an idea and I'd love to see you at your earliest possible convenience."

A week later, he came to my office. Before he got to his formal presentation, he did what any smart entrepreneur would do: He made sure he established a connection with me.

He did this by telling me that I'm a genius. Some people may consider such flattery excessive, but when you're on the receiving end, it's usually okay.

In the most passionate terms, he told me how, fifteen years ago, when he was selling shirts on Venice Beach and barely making a living, he had read a copy of *The Art of the Deal*. He said it had changed his life.

"If that's so," I said, "why haven't you given me twenty percent?"

He laughed heartily. I knew he was setting the table, but he was setting it brilliantly. I was impressed.

Then he told me his idea for *The Apprentice*—a series set in the jungle of New York City, the toughest jungle of them all, where people tear each other apart just to get an inch ahead of the competition.

His idea was terrific: Have sixteen people compete in a televised thirteen-week job interview, where the winner gets to become my apprentice. Whoever won would get a six-figure job at The Trump Organization for one year—maybe longer, if he or she was worth it.

What appealed to me most was that the premise of *The Apprentice* would be educational to viewers. People would be able to see how the real business world works and what it takes to survive in it—or to even have a chance to survive in it.

I asked Mark what kind of a time commitment he would need from me.

Mark's words, which I will never forget and will always remind him of, were: "Donald, believe me, the most time we would need is three hours a week."

I can affectionately say that I was a real schmuck for believing that line.

The first few episodes took about thirty hours each. But it turned out I didn't mind. As time went by, I started to realize that this show could be really big, and I wanted to devote the kind of time to it that Mark needed me to give.

When we pitched the project to the top networks for bids, everyone wanted it. They loved the concept. We chose NBC, which also broadcasts my Miss Universe, Miss USA, and Miss Teen USA pageants, so it was a quick and easy deal. Neither side had to be convinced of anything, and from the very first meeting, the relationship has been a strong one. Bob Wright, the chairman of NBC, and Jeff Zucker, president of NBC Entertainment, are the best in the business. They worked hard to promote the show and were rewarded with rave reviews and the best ratings of any new show of the season. I know this sounds like typical showbiz hype, but it's all true.

Once I got used to the time commitment, working on the show came naturally, because, in effect, what I do on *The Apprentice* is what I do in life: I hire people. I fire people. I make things work.

One of my favorite aspects of the show are the dramatic entrances and exits I get to make—from limousines and planes, or into the boardroom. It's good to be the CEO, and it's even better to be the CEO on national TV. It was also great to enlist the services of special guest stars such as George Steinbrenner and Donny Deutsch, the best advertising man in the business, as well as Regis, of course.

When we announced the show to the media in one of the most publicized job listings in recent memory, the reaction was instant and huge. In the first week, we received over 86,000 website hits. Over 70,000 applications were downloaded—the first one from Hamburg, Germany. The tally reached 215,000 before we finally stopped counting. This might have been the biggest job application in history.

Fortunately, Mark and his team knew what they were doing. After reviewing the twelve-page applications and videotapes required of

The Apprentice *auditions in August 2003. I'm greeting these brave people in front of Trump Tower.*

prospective contestants, ten casting directors and five assistant casting directors studide the materials further, narrowing the field to those deemed strong possibilities.

Their screening process was comprehensive and thorough. In the spirit of fairness, open calls were held in ten major U.S. cities. Tens of thousands of people showed up. In New York City, at Trump Tower, those thousands stood in the pouring rain for hours just to get a few moments of consideration. Obviously, most of them didn't make it, but they've got what it takes to succeed because they've got the guts to go for it.

Seeing their enthusiasm really revved me up for the show. It also bowled me over. I thought to myself, *All these people want to work for me?* It was incredibly flattering. Then again, I doubt those people knew what they might have been getting themselves into. I heard through the grapevine at my office, on one particularly rough day, that the name for *The Apprentice* competitors who didn't win spots on the show was "The Lucky Fifteen."

There were some amusing moments before we began taping. Mark Burnett brought his adoring father, Archibald, to visit one day. After meeting me, he said, "You're much more handsome in person than I would have thought. Maybe you don't photograph so well. Good luck with the show." Mark quickly interjected that his father was from Scotland and tended to be on the blunt side. I think he's terrific.

Mark is a lot of fun to be around—the British equivalent of a Green Beret. He has no fear and tremendous positive energy, which ismy idea of a great leader. We're both big Neil Young fans, so one night, I took him to a concert at the Taj Majal in Atlantic City and introduced him to Neil backstage. Then we went to Naomi Campbell's party in New York City.

I always made a point of mentioning *Survivor* when I introduced Mark to people, but later I realized I was getting some confused looks when I did it, particularly from a Chinese poker winner we met at the

Taj Majal. It took me a moment to figure out that *Survivor* probably isn't on TV in China. The poker winner thought Mark was a cancer survivor and didn't know what to say.

When the crew of the show first appeared at Trump Tower, they created a bit of a buzz. Our ordinary routine was altered by just their presence. It was unusual to see all of those cameras. But within a couple of weeks, it became part of the routine. Jay Bienstock and Kevin Harris, two of Mark Burnett's producers, became fixtures of our organization. Then NBC executive Jim Dowd became a regular. If anything, it was when they weren't around that it seemed like something was amiss. They were never an imposition, and we even missed them when taping was over.

Unlike a scripted movie or TV show, *The Apprentice* that you have seen on NBC is pretty much the way it was behind the scenes. That's the idea—behind the scenes is in front of your eyes. Right away, I can hear you saying, "But we heard the boardroom was a set, and not your boardroom at all." That's true, but the only reason we built another boardroom was because my own boardroom at The Trump Organization is in constant use, and having a film crew in it every week for several months would have disrupted my business. So we built a replica on the fourth floor of Trump Tower. The reception area was also built there because the comings and goings of the sixteen apprentices and a TV production crew would have been a disturbance to our employees and our guests, some of whom may not have been expecting a close-up.

The set was built in Trump Tower so I could take an elevator and be there in fewer than two minutes. My regular business schedule is hectic, so traveling to and from an off-site location could have caused problems. Using the space we had on-site proved to be a good decision.

The living quarters for the sixteen applicants were also built on the fourth floor, and the equipment necessary for filming was installed there. It was an amazing setup, with sound rooms, tech rooms, lights, cameras, and what seemed like miles of cables. When I first saw it all, I realized the immensity of the preparations that went into this show, with designers, decorators, technicians, assistants, producers, and directors all working like mad. At any point, there could be twenty-eight cameras going at once. This was a big operation.

One day after seeing this, I paused silently for a moment. What if the show was a flop? All this work, all this energy . . . well, it just had to work. And I was determined to do my best to make it a hit.

The reassuring thing was that I didn't have to act. That gave me some comfort. Mark Burnett told me that my value to the show would be in just being myself. Is there such a thing as acting like yourself? I don't know, but I try not to think about it. I'm just myself.

I didn't have to read any scripts or learn any lines. Despite having a great memory, I don't have time for that, anyway. Mark would apprise me of the assignments for the applicants each week and we'd go from there. I enjoyed the spontaneity of the process, because we don't rehearse episodes in our daily business life. What happens, happens.

What went on in the boardroom or anywhere else was not fabricated in any way. If it seemed dramatic, that's because business *is* dramatic. There's nothing boring about it. There's nothing passive about it, either—even for viewer.

Seeing the eagerness and anticipation of the sixteen winning applicants was a rush in itself. I never used the word "contestants" in describing them, because this was not a game. People who think their jobs are a game aren't people I want to have around. A lot of these people already had lucrative positions or businesses of their own, so they weren't in it merely for some prize money. We made sure they were all serious about learning something not only after the process but during it. This also ensured that each applicant would be a winner, no matter what the outcome of their quest turned out to be. How many other reality shows have you seen that has only winners? That was another reason *The Apprentice* was so appealing to me. There would be no losers in this win-win situation. My kind of show.

I know what you're thinking. *But you fired fifteen people!* Yeah, but look what they got to do. Look what they got to see. Look what they learned.

All of the tasks required of my would-be apprentices required negotiation skills of one type or another. I was particularly interested in the way the applicants approached the task of achieving maximum savings from a list of items we told them to buy. Items ranged in value from $10 to $550. The highest-ticket item thatd could be discounted was a luxury golf club, a Callaway driver. The winning team homed in on this item. The losers spent their time trying to buy gold, a relatively fixed-price commodity. The winning team learned an essential lesson in negotiation and business: If you win on the big point, you don't sweat the minor ones.

The sixteen applicants quickly became people I liked and cared about—in the way a boss cares about his employees. They were all dynamic individuals with a lot on the ball. It wasn't easy to fire any of them.

Heidi Bressler, 30, an account executive from Philadelphia, Pennsylvania. Heidi is strong, and she kept her objectives in focus in her dealings. She used her account executive background to her advantage in keeping herself balanced.

Jason Curis, 24, a real estate entrepreneur from Detroit, Michigan. Jason has a lot on the ball, but he's young and a little rash. For those of you who missed the episode, Jason cut me off, in mid-sentence, in the boardroom. You *never* interrupt the boss in a meeting. You *never* interrupt the client in a meeting, either. But he will continue to learn and achieve.

Katrina Campins, 24, a real estate broker from Coral Gables,

Florida. Katrina is very accomplished already as a broker, which is a different scenario from that of being the president of a company. I think she will continue to prove herself in her field, possibly becoming an entrepreneur. She will be a success in life.

David Gould, 31, a health care venture capitalist from New York City. David has an exceptional educational background, with both an MBA and an MD, but business is not yet his forte. He surprised me in the first episode when he said salesmanship was not one of his skills. Why volunteer any deficiency? He was the first to be fired.

Jessie Conners, 21, owner of a chiropractic marketing and management company from New Richmond, Wisconsin. Jessie was an interesting mixture of sophistication and innocence. She competed like an experienced player, then did herself in by taking unnecessary abuse from a colleague. You've got to fight back if you want to be successful in business. But don't underestimate her.

Bowie Hogg, 25, an account executive at FedEx, from Dallas, Texas. Bowie has great determination, but when it came to selling, he fell short. He learned a lot, and I'm confident he'll be successful in his career.

Kristi Frank, 30, a real estate broker and restaurant owner from Bel Air, California. Kristi knows a lot about the real world in many ways, due to her business experience, but her failure to stand up for herself showed a lack of one hundred percent focus on her immediate goal. She will do well for herself if she focuses more.

Kwame Jackson, 29, a Harvard MBA and investment manager at Goldman Sachs, from New York City. He is smooth and collected, and will do what is necessary to succeed. Kwame raised some eyebrows when he signed basketballs at Planet Hollywood, implicitly suggesting to customers that he was famous. Was it unethical? When you're desperate, you sometimes have to push the envelope. Kwame was on a desperately failing team. His judgment wasn't admirable, but I don't think he crossed the line: He was supporting his team members.

Amy Henry, 30, a manager at a high-tech start-up in Austin, Texas, who owned millions of dollars in options and lost it all in the dot-com bust. Amy is extremely bright and has great spirit, team and otherwise. I don't think much can get her down, and she will excel.

Troy McClain, 32, a mortgage lender in the insurance business and a real estate developer, from Boise, Idaho. Troy is optimistic and realistic at the same time. It's a great combination, and I expect him to do big things. Plus it takes a brave man to have his legs waxed. That showed me how much he really wanted the job.

Tammy Lee, 36, a stockbroker at Merrill Lynch in Seattle, Washington. Tammy's experience gives her a realistic view of the world. She watches out for herself and keeps her goals clear. Her strength is one of her greatest attributes, and it will help her throughout her career.

Bill Rancic, 32, founder of cigarsaroundtheworld.com, which he started from his studio apartment in Chicago, Illinois, and turned into a multimillion-dollar business. Bill is a good guy with a great future and has already proven his entrepreneurial skills. He's a careful thinker, serious about his endeavors, and a good bet to achieve the results he seeks.

Omarosa Manigault-Stallworth, 29, a political consultant from Washington, D.C., who worked in the Clinton-Gore administration. Like Madonna, she needs only a first name. Omarosa is the most articulate of the group. She's got a lot of fight in her and self-confidence that will serve her well. If she'd been working on Gore's presidential campaign, he would have won.

Sam Solovey, 27, cofounder of an Internet media company, from Chevy Chase, Maryland. He lasted only until the third episode, but even that seemed like an eternity to some viewers. Sam was the smartest annoying character on TV since Howard Cosell. He is likely to either take a company down in flames or create an IBM. I think he's got a lot of talent, and as long as he learns how to use it correctly he will do great things. I can't believe he proposed marriage on TV. His future wife looks great, but he forgot to ask for the prenup, and I hope he won't ever need one.

Ereka Vitrini, 27, a global marketing manager for Clinique, who learned her business skills working in her family's pizzeria in New York City. Ereka has terrific spirit and a good amount of fortitude. She's not afraid to voice her opinions, and that's crucial.

Nick Warnock, 27, a salesman for Xerox who launched an Italian ice business in Bayonne, New Jersey, and now lives in Los Angeles. Nick is a savvy guy who tries to cover his bases. He is industrious but needs to focus on exactly what is going on around him. His tenacity will see him through.

They were all great, even Sam. What I found interesting was the shifting dynamic of the group and their interplay, with its changing patterns and alliances. That's the way business teams function.

As everyone saw, the women dominated the men at first, and it made some people wonder whether women are superior at business. I believe we're all equal, except in one respect: Women still have to try harder, and they know it. They will do what they have to do to get the job done and will not necessarily be demure about it.

A lot of people were surprised when I decided to lecture the women about the way they were using their sex appeal. They used it successfully at first, but I knew that would not always be the case. It works, and then it doesn't, and I didn't want them to fall into a trap.

All the women on *The Apprentice* flirted with me—consciously or unconsciously. That's to be expected. A sexual dynamic is always present between people, unless you are asexual.

As a result of *The Apprentice,* several of my esteemed colleagues at The Trump Organization have become TV stars. I was joined in the board-room every week by George Ross and Carolyn Kepcher. They did for *The Apprentice* what they do for me every day—pay attention to the

At Planet Hollywood in Times Square with George Ross and Carolyn Kepcher.

details, see the big picture, and give me excellent advice. When I told them I wanted them to appear on the show with me, unscripted and unrehearsed, they approached it just like any other job assignment, with thorough professionalism and astute attention, and they came across as authentic because of that.

I chose Carolyn, an executive vice president and the director of one of my largest properties, because she's shown a lot of smarts over the years. George, an executive vice president and senior counsel, is a shrewd, tough guy with brains—he doesn't put up with nonsense from anyone.

My executive assistants Rhona Graff and Robin Himmler are also featured regularly, and even though they have high-stress jobs, I think you'll agree they look anything but stressed on TV. My executives Allen Weisselberg, Charlie Reiss, Norma Foerderer, and Tom Downing also made appearances, and Bernie Diamond appears four times. Whenever I make a big hiring decision, these people are involved, so it was only natural for me to include them in choosing the apprentice.

The only person I had to coax into appearing was my vice president and personal assistant, Norma Foerderer. She prefers being "the power behind the throne" and didn't want to be in the limelight, but I finally convinced her.

I've been asked how much the success of *The Apprentice* will mean to my business. My pay per episode, while substantial, does not, for me, mean very much. It is nowhere near what the stars of *Friends* rake in. The real value is in the free advertising and publicity The Trump Organization has been receiving. I can't put a monetary value on that. Before *The Apprentice,* the use of my name on a building was worth untold millions of dollars. That value sure has not gone down. I'm told that *The Apprentice* is the highest-rated show featuring a nonacting businessman in the history of television. When TV viewers think of business in America, a lot of them are going to be thinking about The Trump Organization.

We're already at work on the second season, to premiere in the fall of 2004. For those of you interested in applying and winning, here are the four essential qualities I'm looking for in an apprentice:

1. *An outstanding personality.* Someone who makes everyone feel comfortable. No matter what you're doing in business—selling, buying, negotiating, analyzing, or managing—this may be the most essential trait. You've got to be able to connect with the people you encounter, every hour, every day.
2. *Brains.* Not book brains alone, but street smarts as well. That combination, properly used, is a winner.
3. *Creativity.* The ability to see beyond the obvious, to think unpredictably and imaginatively, to make connections others might not envision. This is perhaps the hardest quality to develop—you've either got it or you don't. But you can be creative in different ways. Jeff Zucker is a creative TV executive. Derek Jeter is a creative shortstop. If they switched jobs, they might not be as creative in their various fields.
4. *Loyalty and trust.* Absolutely required traits. Unlike creativity and brains, any person can possess these qualities, so if you lack them, you have no one to blame but yourself.

Let's suppose, out of the hundreds of thousands of applicants, you're selected. Let's suppose you actually win. You become famous for fifteen minutes (or perhaps more) and bag a $250,000-a-year job at The Trump Organization.

Then what?

I titled this book *How to Get Rich* because whenever I meet people that's usually the first thing they want to know. From reading these pages, I hope you've gained a sense of what it takes, how to live your life in the way most likely to result in a vast fortune. Unless you win the lottery or have a bonanza at one of my casinos, you're not going to get rich purely through luck. You'll have to work for it, and I've tried to show you how.

My ideal goals are success with significance. That's worth more than the money. Being paid is nice. In most cases, it is absolutely necessary, and a good scorecard for success, but it certainly isn't the only one. I didn't do *The Apprentice* for the money, even though it has been very profitable.

It feels great to be in a position to make a difference, and that's what I mean when I say "success with significance."

I hope you become rich. And I hope you use your talent to make some kind of positive change in your immediate world.

Whatever your job is, that's your assignment.

Begin now.

You're hired.

Acknowledgments

This book could not have been written without Meredith McIver, a writer of many talents. She served her apprenticeship with the New York City Ballet, worked on Wall Street, and for the past two years has been an executive assistant at The Trump Organization, stationed at a desk outside my office. As you know, my door is always open, so Meredith has heard everything, and she's taken good notes. She's done a remarkable job of helping me put my thoughts and experiences on paper. I am tremendously grateful to her.

Very little happens in my office without Norma Foerderer, who oversees my schedule and has been instrumental in keeping this book project on track in many ways, especially in the coordination of the photographs.

I want to thank my editor at Random House, Jonathan Karp, who asked me to write this book. I first met Jon in 1997, when he edited *The Art of the Comeback*. He spent a lot of time in my office, and one day I noticed he was staring at the carpet under my desk. Finally, he said, "Donald, what's the deal with the space heater?"

I told him that my feet get cold.

Jon said, "We're in *Trump Tower*. It's *your* building. Can't you do something about that?"

It's important to have an editor who asks the tough questions.

I'm also grateful to many others at Random House who worked long and late hours to produce this book in record time: publisher Gina Centrello; associate publishers Anthony Ziccardi and Elizabeth McGuire; executive director of publicity Carol Schneider; director of publicity Thomas Perry; associate director of publicity Elizabeth Fogarty; editorial assistants Jonathan Jao (who did an excellent job with the photos) and Casey Reivich; art director Gene Mydlowski; managing editor Benjamin Dreyer; production chief Lisa Feuer; design director Carole Lowenstein; production manager Richard Elman; production editor Janet Wygal; copy editor Ginny Carroll; advertising director Magee Finn; rights directors Claire Tisne and Rachel Bernstein; and everyone in the Random House sales force, which is the best in the business.

At The Trump Organization, I am surrounded by home-run, grand-slam people: Matthew Calamari, Allen Weisselberg, George Ross, Bernie Diamond, Jason Greenblatt, Rhona Graff, Tony Morace, Andy Weiss, Don Jr., Jeff, Eric, and many more.

Meredith McIver would like to thank Mark Burnett, Richard Casares, Steve Palitz, the Bosworth Family, George Balanchine, Alain Bernardin, Christophe D'Astier, Peter Irigoin, and Richard Irigoin. To my family, you are the best. To everyone at The Trump Organization, it's an honor to work with you. To my officemates Rhona Graff and Robin Himmler, a special thanks for your support. To Norma Foerderer and Mr. Trump, thank you both for making every day an adventure. To Mr. Trump, you are a writer's delight. I will never be at a loss for ideas. Thank you very much.

Appendix

THE TRUMP ORGANIZATION PROPERTIES

NEW YORK, NEW YORK

Trump Tower

The city's most famous contemporary building and its third most-visited attraction (with in excess of 2.5 million visitors annually), this sixty-eight-story bronze glass and polished brass structure is situated on Fifth Avenue and Fifty-sixth Street. Completed in 1983 by renowned architect Der Scutt, it is one of the tallest residential buildings and concrete structures in Manhattan. It also boasts 170,000 square feet of commercial space and 136,000 square feet of retail space and is a center for business, a mecca of style and high fashion, and an elite sanctuary to some of society's most famous and influential people.

Trump Place (Riverside South)

The pièce de résistance of Donald Trump's real estate empire, Trump Place is a ninety-two-acre property fronting the Hudson River that promises to be the most exciting real estate development in Manhattan since the turn of the century. In June 1994, Mr. Trump entered into a joint venture with four of the largest Hong Kong real estate develop-

Trump Tower right after September 11, 2001.

Trump Tower, February 2004.

Artist's rendition of what Trump Place will look like when completed.

ment firms, which have committed $2.5 billion to implement this project. The project's first five buildings are complete, with a sixth tower under construction. The overall project will feature sixteen buildings containing 5,700 residential units and more than two million square feet of commercial space. The construction of a magnificently landscaped twenty-five-acre public waterfront park has also enhanced this property enormously by providing bicycle paths that link Battery Park in lower Manhattan to upper Manhattan.

Trump International Hotel & Tower

This fifty-two-story mixed-use structure comprises a superluxury hotel, residential tower, and world-famous restaurant (Jean-Georges). Located at the crossroads of Manhattan's West Side on Central Park West and Columbus Circle, it was designed by the renowned architect Philip Johnson and completed in 1997. Trump International has broken all records to date, becoming one of the most successful condominium towers ever built in the United States and pioneering the concept of a condominium hotel. The hotel achieved Mobil Five-Star status in its very first year of operation.

Trump Parc

Sold out since its completion in January 1988, Trump Parc is an elegant condominium located on Central Park South. Trump Parc's 347 residential units provide stunning views of Manhattan's skyline from river to river, as well as unobstructed views of Central Park.

Trump Park Avenue

In 2002, Mr. Trump purchased the fabled Delmonico Hotel, located at Fifty-ninth Street and Park Avenue. It is now being developed, in partnership with General Electric, into a state-of-the-art luxury high-rise condominium.

Breaking ground at Trump Place.

With construction workers at Trump Place.

Trump International Hotel & Tower.

Trump Plaza

This luxurious Upper East Side cooperative, completed in 1984, combines 175 residential units with numerous boutiques and privately owned apartments, each with its own private terrace.

Trump Palace

With a majestic facade that commands an entire block of Third Avenue on the tony Upper East Side of Manhattan, this 283-unit luxury condominium, completed in 1991, is distinguished by an illuminated spire that has become a distinctive landmark in the New York City skyline.

610 Park Avenue

The Trump Organization, in partnership with Colony Capital, restored the former Mayfair Hotel into luxurious residential condominiums. Situated on New York's most prestigious avenue, 610 Park residents enjoy the ultimate in services, including great dining in the legendary four-star Restaurant Daniel. They also have the convenience of the world's most exclusive shops, restaurants, and museums nearby.

The Trump World Tower

At ninety stories, this is the tallest residential building in the world and is uniquely located across from the United Nations headquarters. In addition to its prime location and impressive views of the city, the building contains 376 units, with a state-of-the-art spa and fitness center, a world-class cocktail lounge, and, within the near future, a glamorous restaurant. The building was named Best Residential Building in the World by the International Real Estate Federation in 2003.

The Trump Building at 40 Wall Street

The Trump Building stands proudly in the center of New York's Financial District, near the New York Stock Exchange. Originally built in 1930, the building stands seventy-two stories high and offers a vast

The Trump World Tower at the
United Nations Plaza.

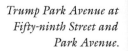

Trump Park Avenue at
Fifty-ninth Street and
Park Avenue.

1.3 million square feet of interior space. Under Mr. Trump's ownership, it has been restored to all the majesty and splendor it once pos-
sessed.

Trump Pageants

In a unique departure from his forays into real estate, Mr. Trump and
the NBC network entered into a partnership for ownership and broadcast rights for the three largest beauty competitions in the world: the
Miss Universe, Miss USA, and Miss Teen USA pageants.

Trump Model Management

Developed by Mr. Trump, Trump Model Management is a modeling
and talent agency. It is managed by the industry's seasoned movers and
shakers and represents some of the most beautiful faces and exciting
talents in the world. It is one of the ten best modeling agencies in
Manhattan.

Wollman Skating Rink

Located in the middle of Central Park, with incomparable views of the
New York City skyline, this is a world-class (and world-famous) ice
skating rink managed by The Trump Organization.

BEDFORD, NEW YORK

Seven Springs

This lush 215-acre estate is the former home of Katharine Graham,
publisher of *The Washington Post*. The magnificent forty-thousand-
square-foot Georgian mansion was designed by celebrated architect
Charles Platt in 1917 and includes a smaller house called Nonesuch, as
well as two cottages, a ten-car garage, a greenhouse, and barns. Mr.

Trump is currently working with a team of international specialists to design a world-class golf course, club, and spa on this magnificent property.

BRIARCLIFF MANOR, NEW YORK

Trump National Golf Club

Nestled among the hills and valleys of beautiful Westchester County, Trump National Golf Club is a world-class club that boasts a 7,200-yard, par-72 course designed by one of the leading golf course architects, Jim Fazio. Currently under construction on the 207-acre property are eighty-seven luxury golf villas and mid-rise condominium buildings.

BEDMINSTER, NEW JERSEY

Trump National Golf Club, Bedminster

In 2002, Mr. Trump purchased Lamington Farm, in the heart of New Jersey horse country, once the home of automaker John DeLorean. Work is currently under way to build a world-class golf course, designed by Tom Fazio, along with fifteen residential super-mansions. Additional plans for this magnificent 525-acre property include a pool, tennis courts, and converting the twenty-thousand-square-foot Georgian-style main house into a spectacular club-house.

LOS ANGELES, CALIFORNIA

Trump National Golf Club, Los Angeles

In 2002 Mr. Trump also purchased the Ocean Trails Golf Course, a magnificent property that fronts the Pacific Ocean for almost two miles. Designed by legendary golf course architect Pete Dye, it is being refurbished and upgraded by Mr. Trump to the world-class standards of his other courses. Luxury estate homes are also being planned for construction on the three-hundred-acre property.

MIAMI BEACH, FLORIDA

Trump Grande Ocean Resort and Residences

Mr. Trump has entered into a partnership with Dezer Properties for an oceanfront development located between Bal Harbour and Aventura. Upon completion, this project will contain three buildings on eleven acres and nearly one thousand linear feet of uninterrupted beachfront. The Trump International Beach Resort was completed in April 2003, with 372 hotel condominium units, ballrooms, a state-of-the-art business center and twenty thousand square feet of meeting rooms. Currently under construction is the fifty-five-story Trump Palace, a residential condominium tower with 267 units. Construction of the third residential condominium called Trump Royale is expected to start in the fall of 2004. These buildings are the tallest residential towers in South Florida.

ATLANTIC CITY, NEW JERSEY

Trump Taj Mahal Casino Resort

The most luxurious casino-hotel ever built, the Taj Mahal is Atlantic City's foremost gaming facility. Opened on April 2, 1990, it has been awarded the prestigious Mobil Five Star award and the AAA Five Diamond award. It has 125,000 square feet of casino space, making it the largest casino in Atlantic City, as well as 1,250 guest rooms, including 237 exotic suites, eleven restaurants, six lounges, 144,000 square feet of convention space, and the sixty-three-thousand-square-foot Mark G. Etess Arena, which seats six thousand.

Trump Plaza Hotel and Casino

Donald Trump's first foray into gaming, Trump Plaza is a five-star, five-diamond casino-hotel located on Atlantic City's famed Boardwalk, adjacent to the Convention Center. This thirty-one-story, 557-room luxury property features sixty thousand square feet of casino space, eleven restaurants, four lounges, and the 750-seat Cabaret Theatre. It has received worldwide recognition as a favored venue to such mega-events as the World Heavyweight Boxing Championships.

Trump Marina

Formerly Trump's Castle, the newly renovated Trump Marina is located on the beautiful Atlantic City Marina waterway. It is a Mobil Four Star casino hotel. Its twenty-six-story hotel tower contains 725 guest rooms, while the principal public area provides fifty-three thousand square feet of convention and exhibit space, nine restaurants, two lounges, and seventy thousand square feet of casino space.

BUFFINGTON, INDIANA

Trump Casino

This elegant casino-yacht, which opened in June of 1996, is nestled in Buffington Harbor, Indiana, just outside of Chicago. Donald Trump's first gaming venture outside of Atlantic City, it is the largest floating riverboat in the world at an astounding 290 square feet long and 76 feet wide.

PALM SPRINGS, CALIFORNIA

Trump 29 Casino

In 2002, Mr. Trump entered into an agreement with the Twenty-Nine Palms Band of Luiseno Mission Indians to manage the Trump 29 Casino, his first foray into gaming on the West Coast.

The Mar-a-Lago Club, Palm Beach, Florida.

PALM BEACH, FLORIDA

The Mar-a-Lago Club

This famous and historic twenty-acre waterfront estate, formerly owned by Marjorie Merriweather Post and E. F. Hutton, was acquired by Donald Trump in 1985. Designed by the renowned Viennese architect Joseph Urban, Mar-a-Lago was designated a National Landmark by the National Trust for Historic Preservation in 1972. It is the only property to receive this distinction in the state of Florida. It was converted by Mr. Trump in 1995 to a private ultra-luxury club that features a world-class spa, renowned dining, tennis, pool, and private beach. The club also functions as an international meeting place for world leaders in government, finance, business, and the performing and fine arts. In 2003, Mar-a-Lago was named by the American Academy of Hospitality Sciences as "the best private club in the world."

Trump International Golf Club

Designed by the esteemed golf course architect Jim Fazio, Trump International was opened in November 1999 and is already a landmark course that features waterfalls and landscapes unique to the state of Florida. In 2002, it was presented with the Five Star Diamond Award "for achieving the highest standards for the greatest golf course in Florida." A spectacular fifty-five-thousand-square-foot clubhouse was also built and based on the Moorish style of the Mar-a-Lago Club.

CHICAGO, ILLINOIS

Trump International Hotel and Tower, Chicago

Mr. Trump entered into a joint-venture agreement with Hollinger International, Inc., owner of the *Chicago Sun-Times* newspaper, to build a luxury, mixed-use development on the site of the current *Sun-Times* building. Located along the Chicago River, the proposed ninety-story, glass curtain–wall building has been designed by the world-renowned architectural firm of Skidmore Owings and Merrill (SOM). The building will contain approximately 2.2 million square feet, with 470 residential condominium units and 200 hotel condominium units, in addition to 125,000 square feet of retail space, more than a thousand parking spaces, and retail shops and restaurants, along a three-story river walk. Residential and hotel condominium sales commenced in September 2003, and it is anticipated that the project will be completed in 2007 as the fourth-tallest building in Chicago and one of the most luxurious buildings in the world.

INTERNATIONAL
TRUMP PROPERTY DESCRIPTIONS

Trump World I, II, and III, Seoul, Korea

Mr. Trump and his Korean partners have built three superluxury, residential high-rise buildings in the heart of Seoul, showcasing the best finishes, amenities, and services. Mr. Trump and his partners are now building a magnificent four-building complex in Busan, Korea, known as Trump World Centum, which will include more than five hundred residential units.

Trump Island Villas at Canouan Island, the Grenadines

The Trump Organization has joined with an Italian financier, Raffles Hotels, American Airlines, and the Moorings Yacht Charters to create a luxury resort and residential community on 1,200 acres of this Caribbean island, located near the prestigious island of Mustique. The resort will open in June 2004 and will contain a Trump International Golf Club. Ultimately, the island will feature 135 villas consisting of custom-designed estate homes to golf villas.

FUTURE DEVELOPMENTS

Trump International Hotel and Tower, Phoenix

This two-building project on East Camelback Road between Phoenix and Scottsdale (across from the famed Biltmore Hotel and Resort) will include a condominium hotel and residences. Situated near some of the most expensive commercial rentals in the area, the project may contain small retail and office components. The designs and relative sizes of the components are currently being developed. The project is scheduled to begin sales in the third quarter of 2004.

Trump International Beach Club, Fort Lauderdale

Located on AIA in Fort Lauderdale, this superexclusive Trump hotel will be situated halfway between chic South Beach and legendary Palm Beach. The designs and relative sizes of the components are currently being developed. Sales for this project are scheduled to begin in the second quarter of 2004.

Villa Trump International Golf Club, Itatiba, Brazil

Located just outside of São Paulo, it includes 150 golf villas, a twenty-seven-hole Jack Nicklaus signature golf course, a Cipriani boutique hotel, twelve tennis courts, 350 residential lots, a Jack Nicklaus golf academy, a clubhouse, and an events center. It contains 1,659 acres, 800 of which are undeveloped.

Behind the Scenes
at The Trump Organization

ABOUT THE AUTHORS

DONALD J. TRUMP is the very definition of the American success story, continually setting standards of excellence while expanding his interests in real estate, gaming, sports, and entertainment. In 2003, he partnered with NBC and executive producer Mark Burnett on *The Apprentice,* which became a smash hit, the highest-rated debut of the season. He and the network are also partners in the ownership and broadcast rights for the three largest beauty competitions in the world.

In New York City, the Trump signature is synonymous with the most prestigious addresses, including the renowned Trump Tower, the Trump International Hotel & Tower, and the soon-to-be converted Delmonico Hotel at Park Avenue and Fifty-ninth Street (Trump Park Avenue). In the gaming arena, The Trump Organization is one of the world's largest operators of hotels and casinos, most notably in Atlantic City, New Jersey, as well as Trump National Golf Club in Briarcliff Manor, New York, and other great courses throughout the United States.

Mr. Trump is the number one *New York Times* bestselling author of *The Art of the Deal, Surviving at the Top,* and *The Art of the Comeback,* as well as *The America We Deserve.* All told, these books have sold millions of copies.

An ardent philanthropist, Mr. Trump is involved with numerous civic and charitable organizations. In June 2000, he received his greatest honor, the Hotel and Real Estate Visionary of the Century award, given by the UJA Federation.

For more information on Donald Trump and The Trump Organization, go to www.trumponline.com.

MEREDITH McIVER was a Ford Foundation scholar and is a graduate of the University of Utah. She lives on the Upper West Side of Manhattan and is a member of The Trump Organization.

ABOUT THE TYPE

This book was set in Galliard, a typeface designed by Matthew Carter for the Mergenthaler Linotype Company in 1978. Galliard is based on the sixteenth-century typefaces of Robert Granjon.